The W......

An Anthology of Modern Poetry in Cornish 1850–1980

Tim Saunders was born in Northumberland and was brought up in Cornwall. His poems have appeared in the anthology *Writing the Wind: A Celtic Resurgence* (1997) and he is the author of *The High Tide – Collected Poems in Cornish 1970–1999*, also published by Francis Boutle Publishers. In 1998 he was made a Bard of the Cornish Gorseth.

Amy Hale is the Research Fellow in Contemporary Celtic Studies at the Institute of Cornish Studies at the University of Exeter. She received her PhD from the University of California and is the co-editor, with Philip Payton, of *New Directions in Celtic Studies* (University of Exeter Press, 2000)

Bobi Jones is one of Wales' leading poets, critics and linguists. He was born in Cardiff in 1929 and educated in Wales, Ireland and Québec. From 1980–1989 he was Professor of Welsh at the University College of Wales, Aberystwyth.

Tim Saunders

The Wheel
An Anthology of Modern Poetry in Cornish 1850–1980

edited by Tim Saunders

with a history of the Cornish Revival by Amy Hale

foreword by Bobi Jones

Francis
Boutle
Publishers

First published by Francis Boutle Publishers
23 Arlington Way
London EC1R 1UY
Tel/Fax: (020) 7278 4497
Email: fbp@francisboutle.demon.co.uk

ISBN 0 9532388 7 3

Printed in Great Britain by Redwood Books

Acknowledgements

I would like to thank the poets and their families for permission to include their poems in this book. Every effort has been made to contact the authors and I apologise to those I failed to trace. I would like to thank the editors of journals and earlier collections in which many of these poems first appeared. These include *Celtia*, *Cornish Nation*, *The Cornish Song Book*, *Kernow*, *An Lef*, *An Lef Kernewek* and *Old Cornwall*.

Finally, I would like to thank the Grand Bard, Ann Trevenen Jenkin (Bryallen) and Treve Crago for providing biographical information. To them, my special thanks.

Tim Saunders, November 1999

Contents

Foreword

Bobi Jones

This book, I suppose, must be a sort of phenomenon. It shouldn't really be here. I have difficulty in thinking of anywhere else in Europe where anything of its ilk can actually be found. It stakes the strongest claim I have yet seen for recognising Cornwall as a fully-paid-up member of the modern national cultures of Europe, reflecting something really and truly remarkable.

Perhaps the word 'resurrection' is not too inaccurate a term to express what has taken place.It is more than just a 'revival', as that can reflect a revivifying where there is already some glimmer of life. But this is a fully fledged return from the dead. And with the phenomenon of 'resurrection' there goes a sort of spirit, an attitude to life and poetry that is original and special. We feel in reading the poetry in this collection that we share in quite a different energy and purpose from that prevalent in street-wise, perhaps somewhat jaded, cultures that have never experienced an almost successful, yet invigorating, threat to their very existence.

The anthology begins in the 'gap' between authentic late medieval Cornish literature and the genuine modern revival. This was an antiquarian 'gap', but nevertheless a significant one. It was in a way pre-revival and eventually lapsed into scholarship. Led by William Scawen, who was followed by his nephew John Keigwin, William Rowe and notably William Gwavas of Paul, this 'gap' group reached its literary zenith with Nicholas Boson, and its scholarly zenith with William Borlase in the following century. The last poet before this group was James Jenkins of Alverton, Edward Lluyd's assistant during the important visit made by that fine Welsh scholar to Cornwall in 1700.

The new period begins in the first decade of the twentieth century with the father of the Cornish Revival, Henry Jenner. But the present anthologist, Tim Saunders, picks up this new story a little earlier, in the nadir of the Cornish tradition during the nineteenth century section of the 'gap' with two most interesting antiquarian specimens – a pair I have encountered for the first time in this collection. Following them, Jenner himself at the beginning of the twentieth century was a serious Cornishman and his *Handbook of the Cornish Language* of 1904 was a rallying cry for a pioneering period. He was the Sir John Rhys of Cornwall. His successor, perhaps the greatest Cornishman of all time, Robert Morton Nance, was the Sir John Morris-Jones of Cornwall. Apart from his substantial scholarship and immense leadership, Nance, a Cardiff Cornishman (I am proud to say) was a genuinely sensitive poet who wrote verse at a level higher than as an 'exercise' or 'service' to the cause. Cornish-language poetry had now come to stay. The pioneers were followed by another pair of enthusiasts: A.S.D. Smith (Caradar), who apart from his scholarship wrote creatively, particularly successfully in the 8,000 line composition *Trystan hag Ysolt*, and Edwin Chirgwin who seems to have moved Cornish literature into a new modern gear.

Now we have reached our contemporaries, and a remarkable pair– E.G.R. Hooper and Richard Gendall. They have provided us with a body of verse of fine quality; and with them we feel safe. There is now a solid literary base for the future. Cornwall now has the confidence and mental energy to do more than just preserve itself. It can think creatively and feel creatively in its own tongue and forms, with something valuable to say about the diversity and fruitfulness of life, that is of universal significance.

Two younger writers, Tony Snell and Nicholas Williams, have enhanced these energies considerably. If I may be excused for developing my Welsh comparisons further, Nicholas Williams, the well-known scholar, is also the T. Gwynn Jones of Cornwall – polished, classical, rather conservative, soundly rooted in medieval romanticism, whereas Tony Snell is the R. Williams-Parry of Cornwall – more restless, venturesome, conscious of the modern period in style, theme and tone. He, I presume, has provided the anthologist with the title of this volume, in his beautiful poem '*An Ros*'.

The anthologist himself is an 'almost-reformed' but never subdued rebel, a spiritually minded Marxist, who cannot conform completely even to the rigours of the left. But with his poetic roots in Richard Gendall and Tony Snell and a host of others, Tim Saunders has come to the present task with catholicity of taste and generosity of spirit. And he has now for some time been, like Nance, a Cardiff Cornishman.

I would like to mention something further regarding the Welsh connection in all this. There are deep links between the two countries which I hope will be made even firmer by this present anthology. Two Welshspeaking Welshmen, D.R. Evans and D.H. Watkins, who made a considerable contribution to Cornish life, are appropriately represented here. But of course, the Cornish connection goes back a very long way. The early literature (with the Tristan tale and the Geraint romance) reminds us of our common heritage. These references to Cornish 'heroic' figures remind us too that influences were far from being one-sided. The figure of Arthur also (probably, in my opinion) was a Welsh borrowing from Cornwall. Then the huge parallel movement of the saints was a shared experience, and again not only one-way traffic. Saint Samson, according to Doble, 'the chief figure in the evangelisation of Cornwall' was probably from Gwent. But numerous other saints, such as Meriadoc, Sulien and Tysilio, Cyngar, Docco, Nectan and the children of Brychan were part of this great pan-Brythonic movement. Some, such as Nonnita, Decuman, Ciwa, Cybi, Padarn, Crannog and Cadog are mentioned in the important Vespasian Calendar derived from Monmouth Priory. In this same document it is noteworthy that the majority of the saints lives included have a shared Welsh-Cornish significance. But what is more intriguing still is the important Latin-Cornish glossary, with some admixture of Welsh forms, found in that same remarkable manuscript. Monmouth is an important and permanent bridge between the two countries.

When we move on from medieval times into the Tudor period we find yet more connections. I have already mentioned the immense figure of Edward Lhuyd. A worthy successor of his was Robert Williams of Rhydycroesau who published his *Lexicon Cornu-Britannicum*, subtitled *Gerlyvr Cernewec*, in 1863. The finest of the Medieval Cornish dramas, by the way, *Beunans Meriasek*, was preserved in Wales and turned up in the Hengwrt in 1869. Another valuable manuscript, John Tregear's translations of twelve homilies c.1560, considered to be 'the longest piece of Middle Cornish prose', was preserved in Flintshire and discovered in 1949.

The Romantic movement of the end of the nineteenth and the beginning of the twentieth century was another momentous shared experience. The Gorsedd exported to Cornwall has had a considerably more useful impact comparatively in Cornish culture than in Wales. This anthology also includes the Cornish adaptation of the Welsh National Anthem – also borrowed by Brittany. There are occasional echoes in the verse included here of the Welsh cynghanedd, and even of the stanza-form englyn.

Caradar is a noteworthy example of this reciprocal relationship. Primarily a Cornish scholar and writer, his contribution to the Welsh cultural revival was considerable. He learnt his Cornish from Henry Lewis' *Llawlyfr Cernyweg Canol*. But every cultured Welsh person knows of his *Welsh Made Easy*, the best learners' introduction to Welsh for more than thirty years. But the thrust of his life was towards the resurrection of Cornish, with his *English-Cornish Dictionary*, the periodical *Kernow*, St Mark's Gospel translated, *Cornish Simplified*, a collection of short stories, *The Story of the Cornish Language*, *How to Learn Cornish*, a translation to Cornish of the Welsh version of *The Seven Sages of Rome*, the long poem *Trystan hag Ysolt*, a translation of the *Mabinogion*, and an excellent edition (with Nance) of the Middle Cornish texts. I was interested in reading his short story *Tremenyans Arthur* to note the influence (literal translation in part) of T. Gwynn Jones' *Ymadawiad Arthur*.

I began this foreword by mentioning the word 'resurrection'. No doubt, that term should now be revised. When we realise the full impetus of all this Cornish activity towards the maintenance of diversity in culture and the vigorous opposition to uniformity and monotony, and thus the revival of the very bases of healthy social life, the term that should have been employed is probably '*insurrection*'. As part of all the ongoing activity this present revealing volume will undoubtedly make a not inconsiderable contribution.

Introduction

Tim Saunders

This anthology represents the poetry written in Cornish from the mid-nineteenth century to the end of the 1970s. It will be useful for students in schools and universities, and also for the general public wishing to become acquainted with what has been written in recent generations.

During this time, Henry Jenner and Robert Morton Nance standardised spelling, vocabulary and grammar. Primarily a written language in the period covered in this anthology, Cornish underwent few changes from the 1920s until the 1980s. This book breaks off around 1980 because by then Cornish was becoming a daily spoken language in addition to a learned tongue used for formal and literary purposes. Since then, poetry in Cornish has become very much more varied, both in form and content. With Cornish Studies now becoming a part of the curriculum at all levels of the education system, this is a good moment at which to take stock.

This anthology is the result of a personal quest. It was through poetry that I discovered the Cornish language, and poetry led me further into it. This was a common experience for many people a generation or more ago. During the 1970s, I set out to search for the poetry that had been written in Cornish during recent generations. Some of it had been printed in hard-to-come-by magazines, some as duplicated leaflets, and some left in manuscript. There were poems about love, faith, childhood, fellowship, and any theme you could imagine. Some were written in traditional forms, some adapted poetic techniques from the common European heritage, and some were experiments in free versification.

Many of the poems were long enough in themselves to fill a slim volume. Consequently, I have had to leave out A.S.D. Smith's *Trystan hag Ysolt* and the verse dramas of Peggy Pollard, for example. The poems here both delighted me and were short enough to fit into a collection of this size. Some of these poems have been published in periodicals such as *An Lef Kernewek* (available in several libraries in Cornwall and elsewhere), *Kernow* (the pre-War magazine of that name, available in rather fewer libraries) and *An Houlsedhas* (in a private collection). The collection is only representative of its period in so far as I was aware of the poets whose work I included.

Cornish probably emerged from the parent Brittonic during the fifth century. It is thus a sister to Breton and Welsh, and a cousin to the Gaelic languages of Ireland, the Isle of Man and Scotland. Little apart from glosses, vocabularies, names in records, and passing references have survived from the Old Cornish period, roughly 450–1100 A.D. Nevertheless, the evidence suggests that there was a sophisticated literary language, sustained by clerics as princely patronage declined. Cornish had ceased to be the language of administration by the Middle Cornish period (1100–1520 A.D.). The surviving literature of that time is overwhelmingly poetic, chiefly religious drama.

In the Early Modern period (1520–1850) the use of Cornish declined rapidly. In contrast to Wales, there was no Cornish Prayer Book, and there was no Cornish Bible.The Cornish language became associated with poverty and disenfranchisement. By the beginning of the eighteenth century, Cornish as a community language was confined to parishes in the Shires of Kerrier and Penwith. But still the people sang songs and told stories and there was religious polemic, ballads and political songs. Though the last monoglot, Dolly Pentreath, died in 1777, there were still people with an oral knowledge of the language, phrases and words and prayers, and the vocabulary and intonation of the language have coloured popular speech in English in Cornwall. This oral tradition has persisted to within living memory. The first fresh attempts at original composition in Cornish seem to date from about the middle of the nineteenth century, and so it is probably best to date the Recent Modern Period (1850–) from then. I have found it useful to divide the Recent Modern Period into four phases. In setting the boundaries of these phases I have applied as my most important criterion the relationship between the poet and his audience.

In the first phase, 1850–1920, poets are writing either for themselves or for a few, known, friends. In effect, they are utilising the surviving manuscript and oral traditions in order to develop Cornish as a learned language, to be used in literature and ceremony. The themes of the poetry are, paradoxically, usually very public: patriotism, war and peace, religious faith. The exception is the Crankan rhyme, an unselfconscious and delightfully-crafted little gem of local malice. From the point of view of technique, the poets either generally use the most popular metres from the Middle Cornish period, or else keep to simple accentual techniques. They are re-occupying, and marking the boundaries of, a territory that had been abandoned and allowed to run wild. The man who brought the manuscript and oral traditions together again was Henry Jenner, the grandfather of the Cornish Revival. He based his linguistic standards, in spelling, grammar, pronunciation and vocabulary, on the usage of the eighteenth century. However, he made it consistent and enriched it with insights gained from studying Breton.

Jenner's *Handbook of the Cornish Language* marks the re-emergence of Cornish into public once again. However, he was not the first poet of the Recent Modern period. That honour belongs to Georg Sauerwein (1831–1903), an extraordinary scholar and humanitarian who acted as a link between many of Europe's minorities. Perhaps the most moving achievement of this period was the work of Robert Walling (1890–

1976) who, while in base hospitals in wartime France, produced that beautiful handwritten magazine *An Houlsedhas* (*The West*), a delightful and poignant triumph of the human spirit.

In the second phase, 1921–1950, the Cornish movement created an audience. After the First World War, Jenner was joined by Robert Morton Nance, an artist and maritime historian whose family background had given him incomparably better access to popular culture. Morton Nance was a gifted organiser, who founded the Old Cornwall Societies. He also set up a Cornish branch of the Gorseth, or Order of Bards. He presided over the whole movement for nearly forty years, creating a view of Cornwall that prevailed practically unchallenged in Cornish letters until the 1970s. Popular early industrial culture merged with Romantic, antiquarian images of the Arthurian legends and the Age of the Saints to provide the background against which most of the poets were content to work. Nance modified the standards for grammar and vocabulary to bring them closer to the usage of the high Middle Ages, when the great verse dramas were produced, while retaining many of Jenner's principles regarding vocabulary and pronunciation. Communal issues remain important during this phase, but the poets are now also exploring personal themes of love, loss, and unexpected delight, anger or sorrow. There are attempts at introducing metrical devices from other Celtic languages, as well as adaptation of metres established in English and other Western tongues. The reoccupied land is now being cultivated.

In the third phase, 1951–80, an audience can now in some measure be taken for granted. Cornish has now developed a certain range of stylistic variation, and towards the end of the phase it starts to become a vernacular once more. Poets can address their readers more confidently, combining themes in daring ways, experimenting with metrical forms that compel the reader to consider the familiar in a new way, and making the individual consciousness the major premise of a poem's content. They are also very much more aware of one another, and share a greater measure of common sensibility. In addition, song becomes an important form of expression, attracting both new and established poets. The cultivated land is now being harvested. Richard Gendall (1924–) makes the whole landscape part of his vision. His friend Tony Snell (1938–), a scientist and explorer of cosmopolitan sensibility, assimilates classical Celtic poetic techniques in order to create vivid detailed portraits of personal and communal experience.

The fourth phase, not represented here, begins about 1980, and is not yet closed. Cornish has been developing rapidly, both as a spoken language and as a medium for writing and the most recent poetry reflects this. Yet although there are lively differences of opinion about the proper course for the language in the next century, all are agreed that Cornish is now evolving freely.

A history of the Cornish Revival

Amy Hale

Setting the stage for a Cornish Revival

We can trace the true origins of the Cornish-Celtic revival back to the late seventeenth century, with the first attempts to reinvigorate Cornish while the language was still being spoken. However, the modern movement had its beginnings in the eighteenth and nineteenth centuries. The interest in things Celtic in Cornwall was emblematic of the wider cultural nationalist initiatives throughout the Celtic language speaking world and Europe at the time. These movements placed emphasis on the notion of a unique 'folk' culture and the presence of a minority language. In the Celtic territories, three areas of antiquarian enquiry in particular combined to underpin the formulation of a nineteenth century cultural nationalist platform: language, Druids, and folklore. In all three areas, Cornwall had a great deal to offer.

Early investigations into the Cornish language were made by the Welsh linguist Edward Lhuyd, who visited Cornwall in 1700 to collect what he could of the Cornish language for his groundbreaking researches into comparative Celtic philology. This was the only modern and comparative scholarly research on Cornish undertaken while the language was still in use as a community language and when the category of 'Celtic' was still in its infancy. Yet this initial inquiry into Cornwall's connections to other 'Celtic' regions, though solely linguistic, was to form the cornerstone for further antiquarian studies embracing other ethnographic assumptions about the cultural relationships between peoples speaking Celtic languages.

Also adding to Cornwall's emergent 'Celticity' at this time was the antiquarian research on various types of megalithic structures, very common in Cornwall, that was fuelling seventeenth and eighteenth century speculation about ancient Druidic rites. After the Treaty of Union in 1707 and the emergence of 'Great Britain', Druids were a very popular subject for eighteenth century scholars probing Britain's prehistoric monuments in the hope of a deeper understanding of the institutions and practices of what they considered to be the original British peoples. In this way they hoped to shape an awareness of cultural unity rather than to emphasise difference. Cornwall's wealth of material remains and its ancient British language was a stimulus for scholarship.

In 1754 William Borlase, one of Britain's most respected antiquarians of the time, and who hailed from Cornwall, produced the influential *Antiquities Historical and Monumental of the County of Cornwall*, in which he argued that the megaliths functioned in the rites of the Celts in Cornwall. A revised and enlarged edition followed in 1769. The first section of this massive tome was devoted to the history and religion of the Druids. Borlase felt they were a native British institution, their heavy concentration in Cornwall indicated by the great number of stone monuments there. He seemed quite certain that the inhabitants of Cornwall were the descendants of the original Celtic population of Britain, as evidenced by the Cornish language, and like the Welsh and the Scots of the Hebrides, he argued, they still carried out the remains of Druidic worship in their folk beliefs and practices. Borlase's work was influential and widely read and helped to place Cornwall squarely on the emerging 'Celtic' map.

As the emphasis on 'folklore' as an indicator of a unique cultural identity developed, particularly during the latter half of the eighteenth century, each of the Celtic regions began to cultivate and accentuate aspects of their heritage in order to assert cultural difference. Two of the most influential manifestations of this shift in the eighteenth century Celtic world were the Scot James Macpherson's Ossian legends and the Gorsedd ceremony of Welshman Iolo Morganwg (Edward Williams). Although it is now clear that both of these cultural icons were invented, or arguably in Macpherson's case, embellished, they both served to spark international interest in the traditions and cultures of other Celtic territories, as well as shaping the direction of folklore as a distinct field of inquiry and influencing the development of cultural nationalism.

Folklore collecting and the rise of cultural nationalism are intimately related. Folk songs, tales, poetry, dress, and dance were all considered to exemplify distinctiveness and as the foundations of unique cultures. It is no coincidence that folklore research flourished in areas where there was resistance to an occupying power, such as Finland and Ireland. We shall see later how a cultivation of a folk corpus contributed to the Cornish-Celtic movement in Cornwall in the twentieth century, yet it is crucial to understand how early Cornwall was considered within Britain to be a particularly 'folky' area. The entire concept of 'folklore' at this period rested on the notion of 'survivals', with collectors using primary and secondary sources in their work to preserve the premodern and the primitive. Even before the collapse of the tin and copper mining industry in the late nineteenth century, Cornwall was constructed by the dominant English culture as an especially primitive place, far from civilisation, where survivals of ancient legends and premodern ways of life were still to be found. It is little wonder that some of the earliest, most thorough folklore collecting efforts were completed in Celtic language speaking areas, and within the 'English regions' (as defined by the Folklore Society) some of the earliest were undertaken in Cornwall.

As the idea of 'Celticity' was taking shape, one of the earliest folk icons to draw scholars to Cornwall from throughout Britain and beyond was King Arthur. Interestingly, although Robert Hunt in his 1865 collection of Cornish folklore maintains that Arthurian legends did not largely figure in the corpus of tales told by the Cornish themselves, the romantic associations of Tintagel in North Cornwall, Arthur's supposed birthplace, drew scholars and artists from the mid-nineteenth century onwards. As the Celtic revivals in Cornwall and elsewhere began to take shape, Arthurian lore would become a primary signifier of Cornwall's Celticity.

The earliest phases of the Cornish Revival

Although there were clear signs that a Celtic revival could happen in Cornwall, the goals of such a movement were not articulated until there was an appropriate framework in place. This framework came with the activities of the umbrella organisation serving the pan-Celtic movement at large: the Celtic Association. It was within this group that Cornish activists first laid down the platform for giving form to their particular, sometimes idiosyncratic, visions of 'Celtic' Cornwall. In 1901 L.C. Duncombe-Jewell formed the Cowethas Kelto-Kernuak (Celtic Cornish Society). The CKK was the first organisation devoted expressly to promoting Cornwall's Celtic identity on an international level. Duncombe-Jewell presented the aims and intentions of the Society in the May 1902 issue of *Celtia*, the publication of the Celtic Association. He stated that the Society was founded 'for the study and preservation of the Celtic remains in the Duchy of Cornwall.' Four main aims were set out:

1. To preserve from damage and destruction and to study the stone-circles, cromlechs, menhirs, hut circles, beehive dwellings, camps, hill forts, castles, logan and crick stones, crosses, oratories, holy wells, cemeteries, barrows, and inscribed stones.

2. To keep carefully every National Custom and above all the truly Cornish sports of Wrestling and Hurling, by presenting every year a Belt to be contended for by Cornish wrestlers, and inscribed silver Hurling balls to each Parish in the Duchy that will ordain an annual Hurling match on its feast day.

3. To revive the Cornish Language as a spoken tongue, by publishing a grammar and Dictionary of the Language, by printing all Cornish manuscripts not yet printed, by giving prizes for fresh competitions in Cornish, by paying a premium for teaching Cornish to Schoolmasters able to satisfy the Council of their fitness.

4. Reviving the ancient Cornish Miracle Plays and re-establishing the Cornish Gorsedh of the Bards at Boscawen-Un.

For the first time we see here the cultural aims of the Celtic revival in Cornwall expressed in a coherent platform. However, despite support from the many of the leading intellectuals and businessmen in Cornwall, Duncombe-Jewell failed to connect with popular symbols of Cornish identity such as rugby, 'Trelawny' (the Cornish national anthem) and the Cornish dialect of English, all of which were widely recognised at the time. Instead he chose to focus on pan-Celtic icons of Celticity such as kilts, the Gorseth and the Cornish language. He was simply more interested in the world of pan-Celtic politics than in preparing a revolution on the ground in Cornwall. By 1904, his affair with Cornwall and the Celtic revival had ended.

Nonetheless, Duncombe-Jewell's vision was inspirational. Under the auspices of the CKK two important events occurred which shaped the direction of the Cornish movement. In 1904, just as Duncombe-Jewell was making his exit, the CKK along with the publisher David Nutt in London brought out Henry Jenner's *Handbook of the Cornish Language*, the first full Cornish language handbook of the modern era designed for the purposes of language revival. Henry Jenner is today one of the best-known names associated with the Cornish revival – much more widely familiar than Duncombe-Jewell. Born in St. Columb Major in Cornwall, Jenner was a librarian at the British Museum when he developed an academic interest in the Cornish language. In 1875 Rev. W.S. Lach-Szryma, a popular vicar of Newlyn with a passion for Cornish antiquities, asked Jenner to come to West Cornwall to help him collect and study Cornish words embedded in the local dialect in order to prove that the Cornish language had not completely died out. More than twenty-five years later, the CKK urged Jenner to take a more active role when he was drafted by Duncombe-Jewell as language secretary. During the life span of the CKK, Jenner lived and worked in London, but within a few years of the CKK dissolving he moved to West Cornwall where he became more active in Cornish cultural affairs.

Also in 1904, Cornwall was admitted into the Celtic Association as a result of Jenner's stirring speech entitled 'Cornwall: A Celtic Nation' at the Association's annual congress. Cornwall now had the international links that ultimately shaped and inspired the other institutions which have since become central to the Celtic revival in Cornwall. It is often assumed that after Duncombe-Jewell left Cornwall in 1904 the Celtic revival slowed somewhat until after the First World War. This is true in the sense that no institutions were created to foster the movement. However, the original impetus could still be felt and the Celtic Cornish movement really got its second burst of energy with the arrival of Robert Morton Nance, whose vision for the movement was more populist and wide ranging.

Nance is a crucial figure. He was born in Cardiff to Cornish parents in 1873, and though his family lived in Wales, they continued to take an interest in Cornwall. Nance's sister recounts in a biography of her brother's early life how as children in Wales they were fed on a diet of Borlase's works on Cornish antiquities and Hunt's collection of Cornish tales and legends, which ultimately became the inspiration for Nance's dialect work for community theatres, *The Cledry Plays*. His family published a small magazine for which Nance illustrated and wrote, expressing an interest for traditional Cornish themes such as fishing, shipping, and even pasties, at a fairly early age. At eighteen, he went to a Cardiff art school and also spent time in St. Ives, sketching fishermen and boats.

Within two years, he began attending the art school founded by Sir Hubert von Herkomer, the man who designed the Welsh Gorsedd regalia. In 1899 Nance took honours at the Eisteddfod in Cardiff for his painting. His sister speculates that it is through these influences that he became interested in Celtic revivalist activities. In 1898–99, he was also illustrating for Arthur Quiller-Couch's short-lived *Cornish Magazine*, which contained fiction, poetry and antiquarian articles relating to Cornwall. By 1906 Nance had relocated permanently to Cornwall, to the West Cornwall village of Nancledra, where he wrote and produced *The Cledry Plays*. They were the inspiration, he later claimed, behind the Old Cornwall Movement.

In 1919, after the First World War, Nance began calling for a revival of Cornish traditions such as 'guise dancing' (a form of mumming) in local papers. He believed that only through the revival of old customs would the Cornish be able to retain their essential Cornishness and continue to express their cultural 'difference'. In doing this, he was employing strategies that the Celtic Association had used twenty years earlier, and which were being employed successfully in countries throughout Europe. Nance was trying to save and perpetuate the Cornish 'folk soul'.

In 1919 Nance founded the first Old Cornwall Society in St. Ives and drafted Henry Jenner to act as president. The purpose of the Old Cornwall Societies (OCS) was to collect and circulate old Cornish folklore and customs, but unlike earlier societies, not only for antiquarian purposes. They were to provide a foundation on which a future Cornish culture could be built:

It is a society in which lovers of Old Cornwall meet as informally as possible to learn more and more about the traditions of Cornwall, not as dry scientific material for discussion nor even as quaint old stuff that, though amusing enough, has no further use unless to attract 'visitors.' Its members, on the contrary, take a hand themselves in 'gathering the fragments that remain', as having a present value, because it by these alone that the Tradition of the Cornish People can be kept alive, and by these alone can Cornwall be kept Cornish still. Ours is thus, if no more, at least.

The Old Cornwall Movement, as Nance called it, was very successful and Old Cornwall Societies soon replaced antiquarian study groups in many Cornish towns and villages. Nance hoped to foster not just interest in the Celtic heritage of Cornwall as defined by the earlier revival, including the Cornish language, but also in other icons of Cornish identity such as Cornish dialect. From the outset the combination of influences from both Jenner and Nance made the Old Cornwall Movement a fascinating phenomenon. First, it provided a means by which the ideas and symbols of the greater Celtic revival could be synthesised with the popular symbols of Cornishness already current. Second, it signalled a change in revivalist ideology by shifting the focus away from an intellectual to a popular footing. The Societies provided for the first time in Cornwall a focus and population base for a cultural resurgence. In 1928 the Cornish Gorseth was established, again spearheaded by Jenner and Nance. There had been earlier half-hearted calls to form a Gorseth in Cornwall, but it was not until the Old Cornwall Societies brought the Celtic-Cornish movement to greater popular attention that a Gorseth could actually be organised.

Despite the popularity of the Old Cornwall Societies and the interest of the general public in the annual spectacle of the Cornish Gorseth, there were whispers that the movement needed more radicalism. Although Nance's vision was one of action and resurgence, not passive research, the Old Cornwall Movement quickly became associated with the anti-quarianism that he fought so hard against. As early as 1931 there seems to have been an indication that the Old Cornwall Movement was not sat-isfying the original aims of the organisers to promote a living Celtic cul-ture in Cornwall. There was a small note from the 'youth of the movement' in the first issue of volume two of the journal *Old Cornwall* in that year stating that place names should receive more attention and that OCS meetings needed to include more Cornish language conversation. In 1932 the same journal noted the emergence of a new organisation, Tyr ha Tavas (Land and Language), described as the Cornish youth move-ment. A note on its development states that the Old Cornwall Societies were perceived by the public as being of interest only to old people and that this group was organised as a response. Tyr Ha Tavas later declared its dedication to the 'unity of persons of Cornish birth or descent who desire to maintain the outlook, individualism, culture and idealism char-acteristic of our race', and it was part of the group's manifesto to foster communication with other Celtic 'races'. Tyr Ha Tavas produced a journal of its own, written entirely in Cornish, but this society was fairly short lived and only lasted from 1933 to 1939.

From the beginning the Old Cornwall Movement has had to try to rec-oncile conflicting impulses: to serve a growing Cornish ethnonationalist movement working with organisations in other Celtic regions, while pro-viding a forum for more passive cultural pursuits. The two motivations may be incompatible. The Old Cornwall Societies have consistently served as a springboard for other organisations and individuals not able to continue to pursue more politically active interests within the OCS framework and constituency. Yet, even today, the Old Cornwall Societies remain important arenas for expressing straightforward pride in Cornishness in combination with a more activist ethos concentrated on cultural preservation.

The 1950s: institutions and agendas

The 1950s saw an increase in Celtic political and cultural activism in Cornwall and elsewhere in the Celtic world, partly as a result of the reor-ganisation of the Celtic Association under the new working name, the Celtic Congress. Although since 1917 Celtic Congresses were held almost annually, in 1947 the Congress began a restructuring process which greatly contributed to its expansion. After the ratification of a new constitution at a meeting in 1949, the Congress emerged as a much more structured organisation with membership branches in each Celtic region and an annual conference held in strict rotation in each of the

Celtic territories.

Cornish activists recall that the 1950 Celtic Congress, held in Truro, was a turning point for Cornish cultural activity. It afforded the opportunity for Cornish people who had similar ideas about the course of the movement to come together and share their thoughts, both cultural and political, for the first time. The 1950 Congress also served as the impetus for the formation of Mebyon Kernow (Sons of Cornwall), Cornwall's first nationalist party, organised initially to promote Celtic culture in Cornwall as well as to advocate home rule.

The Celtic Cornish movement now had the structures through which to develop a coherent platform of political nationalism as well as to promote creative responses to cultural activism, with annual Congress meetings as a focal point for the branch Congress activities. The yearly event served as a 'display cabinet' for the cultures of each of the Celtic regions and therefore provided an impetus for the development of pan-Celtic expressions in Cornwall. Notably it encouraged the growth of a Cornish-language music scene, short dramas, dance, and the wearing of kilts, which increased in popularity among participants in the movement after the 1950 gathering. The meetings provided a pan-Celtic context and performance forum for these activities and artistic innovations in a way that the Old Cornwall Societies did not.

Yet despite new political and cultural innovations within the Cornish movement in the 1950s and early 1960s the movement did not gain significant popular appeal until the rise of the counterculture in the late 1960s brought about the second wave of the Celtic revival.

The Golden Years

Some activists have referred to the period of the late 1960s and the 1970s as the 'golden age' of the Cornish movement. It was during this time that Mebyon Kernow had its biggest electoral gains, and it was also a time of great creative activity among cultural activists. In the 1970s there was a general resurgence of interest in the Celts, which had the effect of regenerating Celtic nationalist movements as well as inspiring new directions in Celtic music, dance and art. Malcolm Chapman in his book on the Celts notes that the shift toward leftist politics and anti-urban sentiment provided fertile ground for those seeking alternative cultural outlets through the 'Otherness' of popularly envisioned Celticism, in Britain and Europe, and in North America. He cites the renewed interest in fantasy fiction, led by Tolkien's *Lord of the Rings*, almost thirty years after the initial publication of *The Hobbit* in 1937, enjoying tremendous popularity and influencing trends in British youth culture ranging from popular music to alternative spirituality. Chapman has theorised that the Celtic revival of the 1970s derived from a desire of British youth to recreate nineteenth century romantic constructions of the Celt as a reaction to modernity. But in the late twentieth century the mass media, the recording industry, and the festival circuit made Celtic art and music more accessible than before, appealing to a wider audience and open to a stream of stylistic innovations.

In 1971 the first pan-Celtic festivals were organised, and since then have been held annually in Kilkenny in Ireland, and in Lorient in Brittany. Unlike the Celtic Congresses, these festivals were for a more general audience and predominantly functioned as a showcase for performance and art rather than socio-economic lectures. Music and dance were and are major components. These festivals served as the impetus for serious research into dance and music traditions in Cornwall and for forming competitive showcase teams which travelled internationally. In 1978 Lowender Peran, an annual pan-Celtic festival held in Perranporth in Cornwall was launched, and it has developed into one of the most important institutions of the Celtic revival in Cornwall. In addition to drawing artists from throughout the Celtic world, Lowender Peran serves as the primary venue for Cornish artists inspired by pan-Celtic themes. Importantly, it also serves as a forum and meeting place for political and language activists.

Throughout the 1970s and 1980s there was a steady increase in interest in Cornish traditions. Folk/rock groups like Bucca and other more mainstream folk singers such as the internationally acclaimed Brenda Wootton produced Cornish language music with a wider appeal. There was also new interest in Cornish language writing which gave rise to limited circulation poetry magazines and publications. Although during this time the Cornish revival was attracting greater interest and international recognition, it was not until the 1990s that the movement started receiving mainstream attention and support.

The New Golden Age: The 1990s

In the 1990s, as in the 1890s, we have witnessed a new phase of the Celtic revival – the third wave. Rising interest in devolution for the Celtic territories as well as greater interest, and even minor advances in preserving the Celtic languages, has led to an increased awareness of Cornish culture and heritage. While Cornwall has not benefited directly from devolutionary measures in the way that Wales and Scotland have, the devolution campaigns have profited Cornwall by raising the overall profile of its cultural and political 'difference' both inside and outside its borders. Additionally, there are a number of factors, historical, economic, political and technological, which have resulted in a rise in 'national' sentiment, particularly in the second half of the 1990s.

In the late 1990s several significant events raised awareness of Cornwall's Celtic heritage and culture and injected the existing movement with a sense of urgency. First, in 1997, the pressure group Keskerdh Kernow (Cornwall Marches On), organised a high profile march from St. Keverne on the Lizard peninsula to London to commemorate the 1497 Cornish rebellion led by Michael Joseph 'An Gof' and Thomas Flamank. The march, which lasted more than a month, captured the imagination and at various stages thousands of Cornish people took part. A crucial effect of the event was that it highlighted a lack of education about

Cornish history and culture in Cornish schools, and renewed a campaign for a targeted Cornish educational strategy.

Also in 1997 the Celtic Film and Television Festival was held in Cornwall for the first time since its inception. This event had a lasting effect by encouraging local media production, initially for the festival competitions, but also gave rise to a number of local media and film festivals. The high profile nature of the 1997 event also allowed the first bilingual village roadsigns to be placed in the festival environs at St. Ives, Carbis Bay and Lelant. The event challenged the Celtic Cornish revival to aspire to new levels of professionalism and artistic innovation.

In 1998 Cornwall suffered the loss of the last remaining Cornish tin mine, South Crofty. The end of this ancient and most Cornish of industries had a marked effect, mobilising the general populace around a variety of Cornish issues and igniting fresh calls for cultural preservation and economic regeneration. A new pressure group, Cornish Solidarity, emerged from the Camborne-Redruth area, gaining several thousand members. Alongside Mebyon Kernow, Cornish Solidarity called for greater recognition of Cornwall's dire economic situation, its lack of higher education facilities and the steady drift if its young people away from the area.

These events led to a much greater visible expression of Cornish difference in a variety of ways. One indicator of the greater popular recognition of Cornish identity is the marked increase in the use of St. Piran's flags (the white cross on a black background representing the popular saint of tinners) on homes and businesses. The Cornish language is also much more used and recognised. The 1990s have generated more Cornish-language texts (in the widest sense) than at any time in history.

A guide to pronunciation

This guide is a basic aid to reading the poems for those who do not speak the language. It is by no means a complete guide and readers should look for further information in any standard textbook. The guide explains the three systems of writing Cornish used in the anthology: Unified, Jennerian and Traditional/Authentic/Modern. Most of the poets included wrote in Unified Cornish, the system formulated by Robert Morton Nance in the 1920s. The exceptions are: Henry Jenner, L.R.C. Duncombe-Jewell, C.A. Picquenard, J.A.N. Snell (in his poems *Mys Du/November* and *An Helgh/The Hunt*), Georg Sauerwein and Tim Saunders, who wrote in Jennerian Cornish or something close to it. John Davey's poem is closest to the Traditional/Authentic/Modern orthography, and although Richard Gendall originally wrote his poems in Unified Cornish he has recast them in this orthography in the light of the subsequent development of his ideas on the language.

UNIFIED CORNISH

Consonants

- **b** as in 'baker', 'habit'
- **c** usually, like **k**, except before **e** or **y**, when it is like ceiling
- **ch** as in church
- **d** as in date, deer
- **dh** usually, as in that, thither, except at ends of words, when it tends to disappear
- **f** usually, as in fear, trefoil, except at the end of a word, or where mutable consonants are softened, when it is like **v**.
- **g** as in game
- **gh** usually, a strong **h**, except at ends of words after vowels, when it tends to disappear
- **gw** like **g** except before **a, e, l, r, w**, when it is like the sound in Gwendoline
- **h** usually, as in horrid, huge, except before unstressed vowels, when it is often silent
- **j** like the sound in ginger, tending towards that in azure
- **k** like the sound in keep, care
- **m** usually, as in mother, slime, except following a short stressed vowel, like tabmark

n	usually, as in now, ten, except following a short stressed vowel, like hardnosed
qu	like the sound in queen, quarter
r	like the sound in rebel, rate. Is never silent
s	usually, as in sister, save, except before a vowel within a word, or where mutable consonants are softened, when it is like the sound in zoo, amazed
sh	as in shine, mash
t	as in ten, mate
th	usually, as in think, therapy, except at the end of words, when it tends to disappear
v	usually, as in very, cravat, except at the ends of words, when it tends to disappear, and before **l**, **r**, and after **gh**, **s**, **th**, when it sounds like **f**
w	as in water, wet
wh	like **h** followed by **w**
y	like the sound in yet, yarrow

Vowels

N.B. There are no silent vowels. Diphthongs are generally pronounced by running the two vowels together.

	Short	*Long*
a	as in hat, matter	as in West Cornwall braave
e	as in hen, fetch	as in day
i	as in greeting	as in seen
o	as in hot, glossary	as in saw
u	as in hut, cup	as in tool
y	as in hymn, bitter	as in seen

JENNERIAN CORNISH

Consonants much the same as Unified.

Vowels

N.B. There are no silent vowels. Diphthongs are generally pronounced by running the two vowels together.

a	as in hat, matter	**â**	as in West Cornwall braave
e	as in hen, fetch	**ê**	as in day
i	as in pin	**î**	as in seen
o	stressed as in hot, glossary unstressed as in London	**ô**	as in saw
u	stressed as in full unstressed as in until	**û**	as in tool
y	as in carry	**ŷ**	as in mine

TRADITIONAL/AUTHENTIC/MODERN CORNISH

Consonants much the same as in English.

Vowels

a	as in hat, matter	aa, ai, a-e	as in West Cornwall braave
e	as in hen, fetch	e, ea, e-e	as in day
i	as in pin	i, ee ,y	as in seen
o	stressed as in hot, glossary unstressed as in London	o, oa	as in saw
u	stressed as in full unstressed as in until	u, oo	as in tool
y	as in carry	y	as in mine

The Poems

John Davey 1812–1891

Crankan

A grankan, a grankan,
A mean a gowas o vean;
Ondes parc an venton,
Dub trelowza vean.
For Penzans a Maragow,
Githack mackwee,
A githack macrow,
A mac trelowsa varrack.

John Davey 1812–1891

Cranken[1]

O Cranken! O Cranken! The stone that was found was small, beyond Well Field, where three shoots grow from a stone. The Penzance road and Market Jew[2] are fearfully stronger and fearfully fresher, and grow three shoots from a horseman.

Georg Sauerwein 1831–1903

Edwin Norris

Ker Mr. Edwin Norris
A aswon war an nor-vys,
Pup cufdra cuffa cufyon,
Hag yu gwywa, dre henna
Dhe dhon an hanow penna
A Edwyn, hen yu 'aswon'.

Woge lettya dydhyow hyr,
Cafaf hydhew ow dysyr –
Yllyf arte dheugh skrepha:
Mar a pe ow lethyr ber,
Gyfeugh e rag fout amser,
Mar re hyr – coskeugh yn ta!

Lyas houl a yth a ler
Aban dheugh a res ow ger,
Tro my skrephen arta'n scon:
Mar dhewedhes collenwel
Tra ambosys dheugh mar bel
Dhymmo yu meth, y gon.

Dyffry ny vydh powesva
Dhymmo, hep an newodh da
A'gas gyffyans lyen a ras:
Gyfeugh dhymmo, cowydh ker,
Gweleugh vy rageugh war ler,
Dreheveugh vy, ow Syr mas!

Dreheveugh ve arta'n ban
Dh'agas kynse grasow splan,
A fue dhymmo dysquethys,
Pan yn Loundra, 'n agas chy
Ymysk agas ol deilu,
Geneugh kousel a yllys.

Pandra wrussyn leveryl?
Pup tra, ha trao *erel*:
Gerryow wherow, gerryow whek,
Am bup tavas pel po oges –
Ow gul omladh, ow gul cres –
Ogh, an amser lowen, tek!

Georg Sauerwein 1831–1903

Edwin Norris[1]

Dear Mr. Edwin Norris whom I
know in the world, every kindest
kindliness of kindly ones, and,
what is more fitting, to bear the
chiefest name of Edwyn, that is
'know'.[2]

After long days' frustration, I
shall get my desire today – I can
write to you again: should my
letter be short, forgive me for
lack of time, if too long – sleep
well!

Many suns have gone down
since I gave you my word, it is
high time for me to write to you
again: fulfilling so late some-
thing promised you so long ago
is shameful of me, I know.

Certainly, there will be no rest for
me, without the good news of
your most gracious forgiveness:
forgive me, dear comrade, see
me prostrate before you, lift me
up, good Sir!

Lift me up again, to your former
bright graces, that were shown
to me when in London, in your
house amongst all your family,
when I could speak with you.

What did we talk about?
Everything, and *other* things!
Bitter words, sweet words,
about every language far and
near – doing battle, making
peace – oh, the happy, beautiful
time!

Lemmyn ny'm bydh moy nep dra
Hep ow hof a'n dydhyow da,
Cof, ha hireth y'm calon.
Hireth bras, ha hireth down,
Hag yn teffry, doubt hag own,
A dhewyllyf dres an don!

Gwylsough'n wlas – my a'n aswon —
G'las an meyn a-ugh an don,
G'las lowene, tekdra, marth,
Wodheugh why, pa'n g'las a'n pow!
G'las Tre-pen-pol, g'las Kernow!
Yno ny a a warbarth!

Lemmyn gwylyow lowena
Yn agas tre, yn Loundra,
Dheugh why, ha dh'agas teilu:
Blydhen newodh dha yn whyth,
Lowene newodh pup dyth,
Ha hydhew, farwel dheugh why!

Cowyth Ker, dhe Dhen Claf

Cowyth ker, dhe dhen claf
Trist yu pup tra, kyn fe'n haf,
Kyn fe'n houl ha'n stergan glan:
Lemmyn. Kyn a pup tra'n nos
Ny ellough why'ndella mos.
Kepar ha'n houl ha'n stergan
Ma 'gas cufder ynof splan
Gans y wolow y honen
Pan a's cofiaf y'm colon:
Duw a's bynyga pup deyth
Hag a'm gra vy cuf yn wheyth
Dhe skrepha del gon!

Now I have nothing more than the memory of the good days, memory, and longing in my heart. Great longing, and deep longing, and, certainly, anxiety and fear that I will not return over the waves!

You saw the land – I know it – the land of the rocks above the waves, the land of joy, beauty, wonder, you know which land in the kingdom! The Land of Trepen-pol,[3] the land of Cornwall! Thither we shall go together!

May there be festivals of joy in your home, in London, for you and your family: and a happy new year, new joy every day, and today, farewell to you!

Dear Friend, to a Sick Man[4]

Dear friend, to a sick man everything is sad, although it is summer, although it is now sunshine and starlight. Although everything becomes night, you cannot become like that. Like the sun and the starlight your kindness is bright within me with its own light when I remember you in my heart: God bless you every day and give me grace also to write as I know!

Henry Jenner (Gwas Myghal) 1848–1934

Bro Goth Agan Tasow

Vro goth agan tasow, dha flehes a'th gar,
Wlas ger an housedhas, pa vro yu dha bar?
Heb own berh an bresel, dha gaswyr mar vas,
    Ragos di ga goys a skillas.
                Kernow! Kernow! Ny gar Kernow!
                Hedre vedh mor vel fod en e dro,
                Thon 'Onen hag Ol' rag Kernow.

Devedhyans an Matern

Sav aman, Dinas Dew, devedhys yu
    Dha wolow, an roul coth yu tremenes.
Fethes an Escar, taw an Tuller deu,
    An Matern gwir a dhe wosteweth dhes.

Tewlder a wressa kidha fas an bes,
    Trom warnen ny drog-allosow an Nos.
En splander sans Ev a ve devedhes;
    Golow yu'n bes, ha'n matern ny ow tos.

An Vaternes a'n sens war i deulin;
    Matern Maternow, heb bris yu Dha Dron!
Mireugh, coyn rial rag E vegyans gwin,
    Ha'n Werhes worth E vaga a'i deuvron.

Kensyu saw beugh hag asen ol adro,
    Ha bigely 'ga Matern dho wordhya,
Omblegya wra Maternow prest dhodho,
    E vigely gans rohow dho servya.

'Wren E gorona lemmyn? Nynsyu gwres
    E ober; tanow yu E servisy.
En dadn E dreys pan vedh pebtra settyes,
    'Goren adro dhoy dal y whorryans y.

'Wren E gorona gans ower? Nyns yu'n er;
    Garlons a dhevnedh aral rag E ben,
Pan wel is ol an bes en gordhyans mer
    Agan Matern ow roulya a'n Grows-pren.

Henry Jenner (Gwas Myghal) 1848–1934

Ancient Land of Our Fathers[1]

Ancient land of our fathers, your children love you, dear land of the west, what country can compare? Without fear in battle, your warriors so good shed their blood for you. Cornwall! Cornwall! We love Cornwall! While the sea is like a wall about it, we are 'One and All' for Cornwall.

The Coming of the King

Rise up City of God, your light is come, the old order has passed away. The enemy is conquered, the black Deceiver is silent, the true King comes at last to thee.

Darkness had covered the face of the world, heavy upon us were the evil powers of the Night. In holy brightness He was come; light is the world, and our King coming.

The Queen holds him on her knees; King of Kings, without price is your throne! Behold, royal food for his divine nourishment, and the Virgin feeding him with her breasts.

Although only a cow and an ass stand by, and shepherds worshipping their King, Kings ceaselessly bow to him, His shepherds with gifts to serve.

Shall we crown Him now? His work is not done; scarce are His servants. When everything is put under His feet, they will place a crown above His brow.

Shall we crown Him with gold? It is not time; garlands of another substance for His head, when all the people of the world see our King in great glory ruling from the Tree of the Cross.

Lowenen; ottama 'gan matern ny.
     Hedhew a'n dra a wharfo na woleugh.
Ogas dhoy Stevel-Tron heb own deugh-why;
     Maria'n Vaternes a elow deugh.

Dhô'm Gwrêg Gernuak

Kerra ow Holon! Beniges re vo
Gans bennath Dew an dêdh a'th ros dhemmo,
Dhô whelas gerryow gwan pan dhetha vî
Tavas dha dassow, ha dhô'th drovya dî.
En cov an dêdh splan-na es pel passyes;
En cov idn dêdh lowenek, gwin 'gan bês,
War Garrek Loys en Côs, es en dan skês
Askelly Myhal El, o'gan gwithes;
En cov lîas dêdh wheg en Kernow da,
Ha ni mar younk – na whekkah vel êr-ma
Dhemmo a dhîg genef an gwella tra,
Pan dhetha vî en kerh, en ol bro-na;
Dheso mî re levar dha davas teg,
Flogh ow empinyon vî, dhô'm kerra Gwrêg.

An Pemthak Pell

Dhen yu Gwlas an Ahel Mer,
Arhel Kernow, gwidn ha cler;
War e bedn yu basnet splan,
En e dhorn yu cledha dan.
          Gorwyth Kernow, Arhel Mer!

War e scoudh yu costan hir,
Costan Kernow, dour ha gwir;
En tewolgow an bes deu
Golow owr a dhe a Dhew.
          Gorwyth Kernow, 'Gostan Hir!

En owr splan an Pemthak Pell,
Arvow Kernow lel, es gwel
Ages arvow ol an bes,
Mysteryow an Vaternes;
          Onen hag Ol, 'Bemthak Pell!

40

Let us rejoice; here is our King. Do not weep today because of what happened. Come without fear to His Throne Room; Mary the Queen calls you.

To My Cornish Wife

Beloved of my heart! Blessed with the blessing of God be the day that gave you to me, when I came to look for the feeble words of the language of your fathers, and to find you. In memory of that bright day which has long since passed, in memory of a happy day, how fortunate we were! On the Grey Rock in the Wood, which is under the shelter of the wings of the Archangel Michael, who was our guardian; in memory of many pleasant days in good Cornwall, when we were so young – and it's just as pleasant now – and when I came away I brought with me the best thing in all that land; to you I speak your beautiful language, my brainchild, to my dearest wife.

The Fifteen Bezants[2]

Ours is the Land of the great Archangel, the Archangel of Cornwall, fair and bright, on his head is a shining helmet, in his hand is a sword of fire. Guard Cornwall, Great Archangel!

On his shoulder there is a long shield, the Shield of Cornwall, firm and true; in the darkness of the black world golden light comes from God, Guard Cornwall, Long Shield!

In the bright gold of the Fifteen Bezants, the Arms of faithful Cornwall, which are better than all the arms of the world, the Bezants! Mysteries of the Queen; One and all! Fifteen Bezants!

Ema Pemp es Lowenek,
Ema Pemp es Morethek,
Ema Pemp en Nor ha Nev
Len a wordhyans gwidn ha crev;
      Ottans y, an Pemthak Pell!

An Goven
P'rag ethyw an Pemthak Pell,
Kensens arvow Kernow, gwel
Ages arvow ol an bes?
Pyu homma, an Vaternes?
      Lavar dhen a'n Pemthak Pell.

P'rag ethens y Lowenek?
P'rag ethens y Morethek?
P'rag ethens en Nor ha Nev
Len a wordhyans gwidn ha crev?
      Dismeg dhen an Mysteryow.

An Gortheb
Mab Dew gan Matern Tas,
Mab Maria, len a ras,
A ve gennes en bes-ma
Dho verwel, 've Offryn da,
      Onen rag Ol, ragon ny.

Sol-a-bres Mab Dew a dheth,
Ow casa e Vaterneth,
Ha Maria an Werhes
Yu E Vam, an Vaternes.
      Lowena dho Varia,
      Mam Dew ha Maternes dha!

Thera dinerhyans deuweth;
Sans era'n *Genesegeth*;
Deuweth 'berh an *Eglos Dek*
Be Jesu, gans E Vam whek;
      Otta Pemp es Lowenek.

Whes a Woys agan Matern;
Scorjans: Coronyans gans Spern;
Pren an Grows dho vos deges,
Wher an Ancow rag an bes;
      Otta Pemp es Morethek!

There are Five which are Joyful, there are Five which are Sorrowful, there are Five in Earth and Heaven which are full of blessed and strong glory; behold them, the Fifteen Bezants!

The Question
Why are the Fifteen Bezants, although they are the Arms of Cornwall, better than all the arms of the world? Who is this, the Queen? Tell us of the Fifteen Bezants.

Why are they Joyful? Why are they Sorrowful? Why are they, in Earth and Heaven, full of fair and strong glory? Explain to us the Mysteries.

The Answer
The son of God our Father King, the Son of Mary full of Grace, was born in this world to die, as a good Offering, One and All for us.

Long ago came the Son of God, leaving his Kingdom, and the Virgin Mary is his Mother, the Queen. Joy to Mary, Mother of God and good Queen!

There was a welcoming twice; holy was the *Nativity*; twice was Jesus within the *Beautiful Church*, with His sweet Mother; behold Five which are Joyful.

The *Bloody Sweat* of our King; *Scourging; Crowning with Thorns; The Tree of the Cross to be carried, the Agony of Death for the World;* behold Five which are Sorrowful!

De-Zil Pask ha'n *Askenyans;*
Ha *Zil-Gwidn an Speres Sans;*
ha *Ewhellyans* Dama Dew;
Ha'y *Horonyans* gans Jesu;
      Otta Pemp es a Wordhyans.

Gans an Pemthak Pell yu gwres
Garlons agan Arledhes;
Crist, Maria, Myghal El,
Gwitheugh Gwlas an Pemthak Pell,
      Kernow ker, Onen hag Ol!

Can Wlascar Agan Mamvro

'Sedhys war Vor Gorlewen,
Caslan a nerthow garow,
Mamvro sans ragos canyn
Ny, dha fleghes, 'gan canow.
Agan colon ny a's trel
Dhe'n wlas may fuen-ny genys
Ragos gans pysadow lel.

War dhyfyth an mor ha'n don,
Yn tewolgow an bal du,
Ple pynag 'vo dha vebyon
Dhyso-jy yn prederow
Taran mor, gun redenek,
Dhyso-jy yn covathow
Dha gaswer mar golonnek.

Arthur gans marghogyon vas,
Gerrans cref, an amyral,
Lanslot, cans cas a borthas,
Trystan, Gawen, Perseval,
Y res eth yn arvos splan
Dhe whylas kelegel sans
Dre gosow, dre dhowr ha tan,
Mystry agan crysyans.

Yn tewolgow dha dus vas
A vue lel dhe'n wyr grysyans;
Tanow, gwan, y a verwys
Yn un vresel hep sperans.
War Un Badon y codhas
Dha fleghes rag an Ruy

Easter Sunday and the *Ascension*; and the *Pentecost of the Holy Spirit:* and the *Assumption* of the Mother of God: and her *Crowning* by Jesus; behold Five which are Glorious.

From the Fifteen Bezants are made the Garlands of our Lady; Christ, Mary, Archangel Michael, guard the land of the Fifteen Bezants, dear Cornwall, One and All!

Patriotic Song of Our Motherland[3]

Holy motherland, set on the Western Sea, battlefield of harsh forces, we your children sing our songs for you. Scattered over the world, we turn our hearts towards the land where we were born with a faithful prayer for you.

On the desert of the sea and wave, in the darkness of the black mine, wherever your sons may be, they are yours forever; yours in thought of sea's thundering and fern-covered down, yours in memories of your warriors so brave.

Arthur with good knights, strong Gerontius the admiral, Lancelot who bore a hundred battles, Trystan, Gawain, Perceval, they have gone in bright armour to seek a holy chalice through woods, through water and fire, the mystery of our faith.

In darkness your people were faithful to the true faith; few and weak, they died in a war without

Y lyther del dhysquedhas
Na wrussons y dyfygy.

Myghal a'n Garrek Wythys,
Dherag Dew agan Sansow,
Ken a'n venten venygys,
Peran, Sans an tewennow,
Ruan an morrep dyghow,
Ya, Brueg, ha cans erel –
Gwreugh gorwytha agan pow!

hope. On Mount Badon your children fell for the King, and his letter proclaimed that they did not yield.

Michael of the Guarded Rock, our Saint before God, Keyne of the blessed fountain, Piran, saint of the sand dunes, Ruan of the southern coastland, yes, Briock, and a hundred others, guard our country!

L.R.C. Duncombe-Jewell (Barth Glas) 1866–19??

Mychternes, Mychternes an Eleth Dhus!

Pan us 'gan bewnans moel wherow vre,
Hag an treys skith war an fordh difygyans,
Luen ef a berygl; sellys gans guweluans
Dre'n armor veur; agan skovornow, gwae,
Bodhar a gwrys gans lef a gwyns adre:
Pan lowen cellys demythas tristans,
A neb a flehes 'gan pesadow gens:
Pan an gelvinak ole war an bre:
Dus, a Varia, steyr y'th vlew, a dhus!
Ha syns dhe lau, par del am loer gwen,
Avan war agan pennow'n agan ken.
Del welon, dres tubbasnow dybyta,
Dew, ar tir dagrow a welas adrus,
Ha Cryst a marow auch war Grows-an Wra.

L.R.C. Duncombe-Jewell (Barth Glas) 1866–19??

Queen, Queen of the Angels, Come!

When our life is like a bitter bare hill, and
our feet are tired on the road of exhaustion,
full of danger; our sight gazes through the
great coastland; our ears, alas, are made
deaf by the voice of a homeward wind:
when joy was lost and sadness came from
the children of our prayers: when the
curlew wept on the hill: come, O Mary, with
stars in your hair, O come! And hold your
hand, like the white moon, up above our
heads on our behalf. Thus we see, above
merciless thought, God, looking over at the
land of tears, and Christ dying up on Crows-
an-Wra.[1]

C.A.Picquenard (Ar Barz Melen) 1872–1940

An Nef Kellys

Glau a wra. An auhel cref ha lef an mor garow
A gan del wra an ioul yn cres an tewolgow:
Ellas! Tryst ty an nor ha tryst yu an bys-ma ...
Ow dewlagas a wel an Ancou dre bup tra.

Ellas! tryst yu an nos ha tryst yu pup den ol:
My a glew yn Yffarn an enevow a ol
Hythew ha bynary war an Nefow kellys ...
A enevow, lemmyn pel yu'gas gwlas kerrys!

Deu gwir mestr an bys ol a wor an wirioneth
'Lavar th'an golon glan 'Dus dhe weles ow eleth!'
My a glew yn Yffarn an enevow a ol ...
— Creneugh, a why, creneugh a golonow galas!
Ny, caren agan dew ha tavas agan gwlas!

C.A Picquenard (Ar Barz Melen) 1872–1940

The Lost Heaven

It is raining. The wind and the voice of the rough sea sing like the devil in the darkness: woe! sad is the earth and sad is this world … my eyes see death through everything.

Woe! Sad is the night and sad is every man: I hear in Hell the souls which weep today and forever for the lost Heaven … O souls, far away now is your beloved country.

God, the true master of the whole world, knows the truth and says to the pure heart 'Come to see my angels!' I hear in Hell the souls which weep … Quake, quake, hard hearts! As for us, let us love our god and the language of our country.

Robert Morton Nance (Mordon) 1873–1959

Nyns Yu Marow Maghtern Arthur!

An balores, du hy lyw
    Ruth hy gelvyn cam, ha'y garrow,
War als Kernow whath a-vew
    Kyn leverer hy bos marow.

Yn palores, ny a-wor,
    Speres Arthur, mo ha meten,
Whath a-dryg, ha, reb an mor,
    A-wra gwytha Enys Breten.

Maghtern Arthur, dre dha voth,
    Pan us gansa dha balores,
Re-bo gans tus Kernow Goth
    Bys vynytha bew dha speres!

Arta Ef A-Dhe

War scoren noth pren derow py kefer del yn gwaf?
Whath arta mylvyl delen las a-dyf pan dheffo haf!

War dreth segh yn prys mordryg rag scath py kefer dowr?
What arta lanwes mor a dhe, rag gorhel myghtern lowr!

Py kefer houl yn ebron yn tewlder hanternos?
Whath arta golow hanterdeth yn splander a wra dos!

Py kefer Myghtern Arthur? Ny-wor den-vyth an le.
Whath nyns yu marow; ef a vew, hag arta ef a-dhe!

Dynergh dhe Dus a Vreten Vyghan

Myr a Gernow, arta war dha dyr,
    Wosa dek cansvledhen hyr,
Avel fleghes esa kellys pell,

Robert Morton Nance (Mordon) 1873–1959

King Arthur Is Not Dead!

The chough,[1] black its colour and
red its bent beak and legs, is still
alive on the shores of Cornwall,
although it is said to be dead.

We know that the Spirit of Arthur
remains night and day in a
chough, and by the sea guards the
Island of Britain.

Through your will, King Arthur,
since we have your chough, let the
people of Old Cornwall keep your
spirit alive forever!

He Shall Come Again

Where are leaves found on the bare branch of an oak tree in the
winter? But a million green leaves will grow again when the
summer comes!

Where is water found for a boat on a dry beach at the time of
ebb? But the flowing of the tide will come again, enough for a
king's ship!

Where is a sun found in the sky in the darkness of midnight?But
the light of midday will come again in brightness!

Where is King Arthur found? No one knows the place.
But yet he is not dead; he is alive, and he shall come again.

Welcome to Men from Brittany

Look, O Cornwall, at the men of Armorica
on your soil again, returning to you after ten
long centuries, like children that were lost a

Dhes tus Arvor a dhewhel
　　Clew ny, ow-cana pup den ol yn-fen
　　'Kernow bynary! *Breiz da virviken!*'[2]
　　Ny a'n te, nefra ny-vyth ken nep-prys,
　　Brython a-gar Brython bys gorfen bys!

Saws ha Frynk, y'ga breselyow kens,
　A-'gan gwruk bos yskerens,
Mes dre gana un hevelyp can
　　Cas dhynas a neghsyn glan:
　　　　Y gledha pup a-woras yn y won,
　　　　Yn-un-grya 'Brython ny-lath Brython!'
　　　　Ny a-n-te, nefra ny-vyth ken nep-prys,
　　　　Brython a-gar Brython bys gorfen bys!

Deugh, tus Kernow, bys yn gwartha nef
　　Seveugh lowen agas lef,
Ow-tynerghy 'gan kerens Arvor,
　　Es devedhys dres an mor:
　　　　Gwren-ny ambosa, nefra ny-vyth ken
　　　　Es carensa yntredhon bys vyken,
　　　　Ny a-n-te, nefra ny-vyth ken nep-prys,
　　　　Brython a-gar Brython bys gorfen bys!

Yeghes Da dhe'n Myghtern!

Yeghes da dhe'n Myghtern:
　　Dew re'n gwytho rag coll!
Cowetha, dun evyn,
　　Pup orto y nessevyn,
Bys pan vo an balyer gwak oll,
　　　　Tus vas,
Bys pan vo an balyer gwak ol!

Yeghes da dhe'n Myghtern!
　　Pell re-rewlyo warnen!
Owth-eva ha cana,
　　Pan vo genen banna,
Ten aral a-sew pup pen ten,
　　　　Tus vas,
Ten aral a-sew pup pen ten!

Yeghes da dhe'n Myghtern!
　　Eva nep a-dhynargh,
Na nep a-vyn tewel

long time ago! Hear us singing, every man staunchly, 'Cornwall for ever! *Brittany for ever!'* We swear it will never be otherwise, Briton will love Briton till the end of the world!

The Saxon and the Frank, in their by-gone wars, made us enemies, but by singing the same song we completely overcame unnatural hatred. Everyone put his sword in his sheath, crying 'Briton will not kill Briton!' We swear it will never be otherwise, Briton will love Briton till the end of the world!

Come, oh men of Cornwall, raise your voices joyfully to the heights of heaven, welcoming our kinsmen from Armorica who have come across the sea: let us promise that there will never be other than love between us. We swear it will never be otherwise, Briton will love Briton till the end of the world!

Good Health to the King!

Good health to the King: God keep him from loss! Comrades, let us come and drink, every one for his kindred, until the barrel is completely empty, good men, until the barrel is completely empty!

Good health to the King: may he reign long over us! Drinking and singing, when we have a drop, one draught follows another, good men, one draught follows another!

Good health to the King! He who will not drink, and he who insists on being silent when we

Pan ganen mar ughel,
A'y vewnans byner re-bo yagh,
Tus vas,
A'y vewnans byner re-bo yagh!

An Margh Coth

Galargan Vorethek

Yth-esa gwas, hep our yn argh,
Eghan! Govy!
Na-n-jeva da y'n bys saw margh.
Eghan! Govy!
Ascornek o, hag uthek coth,
Oges ga dek-warn-ugans bloth.
Ogh, tru, dun kynyn oll warbarth eghan, govy!

Whel cref a-borthas war an tyr,
Eghan! Govy!
Ow'cones lyes bledhen hyr,
Eghan! Govy!
Sconya nep eghen whel ny-wruk,
Pup saw dh'y allos ef a'n duk
Ogh, tru, dun kynyn oll warbarth eghan, govy!

Bo tenna mon, bo don meyn pos,
Eghan! Govy!
Bo, dhodho fron ha dyber, mos
Eghan! Govy!
Dhe varghas, bo melyn mar pe,
Y-kemeras pup-oll yn gre.
Ogh, tru, dun kynyn oll warbarth eghan, govy!

Mes dhe bup tra, ha drok ha da,
Eghan! Govy!
Y'n gorfen yma dewedhva,
Eghan! Govy!
Yn-danno y ysyly gwan
A gamma, scant na-saffa 'ban.
Ogh, tru, dun kynyn oll warbarth eghan, govy!

Yth-e ynweth y gen yn cam
Eghan! Govy!
Saw ma na-bortha, malbew dam;
Eghan! Govy!
Ha war an prys, dre hender bras,

sing so loudly, throughout his
life may he never be healthy,
good men, throughout his life
may he never be healthy!

The Old Horse

A Mournful Dirge

There was a man, without money in a
coffer, *Alas! Woe is me!* who had noth-
ing in the world but a horse. *Alas! Woe
is me!* Bony it was and fearfully old,
nearly thirty years of age. *O pity, let us
come and all sing together, alas! Woe
is me!*

It did hard work on the land, *Alas! Woe
is me!* serving for many a long year,
Alas! Woe is me! without refusing any
kind of work, and carrying every load it
could. *O pity, let us come and all sing
together, alas! Woe is me!*

Drawing manure, or carrying heavy
stones, *Alas! Woe is me!* or, going in
bridle and saddle, *Alas! Woe is me!* to
the market or the mill taking everything
joyfully. *O pity, let us come and all sing
together, alas! Woe is me!*

But eventually an end comes to every-
thing, *Alas! Woe is me!* whether good
or evil, *Alas! Woe is me!* and its weak
legs bent under it so that it could not
stand up. *O pity, let us come and all
sing together, alas! Woe is me!*

And its back also became crooked,
Alas! Woe is me! so that it could not
carry anything at all; *Alas! Woe is me!*
and it fell dead of old age right there on
the field. *O pity, let us come and all
sing together, alas! Woe is me!*

Y'codhas, marow, war an pras.
Ogh, tru, dun kynyn oll warbarth eghan, govy!
An gwas, pan welas an droklam,
Eghan! Govy!
A-gryas, 'Clamder yu, hep nam!'
Eghan! Govy!
Ha pluf a loscas ryb dh'y dron,
Ha whystra, yn y scovarn, son.
Ogh, tru, dun kynyn oll warbarth eghan, govy!

Mes dall ha bodhar o, y ben
Eghan! Govy!
Na alsa sevel, nag omgwen,
Eghan! Govy!
Ena an gwas, ow studhya down,
A-brederas 'Ny-n-ladha nown!'
Ogh, tru, dun kynyn oll warbarth eghan, govy!

'Ny-n-ladha whel; ny-n-ladha gu;
Eghan! Govy!
Rag fowt a anel marow yu!'
Eghan! Govy!
Y-halwas ena dh'y wrekty,
'Heth dha vegynnow dhymmo-vy!'
Ogh, tru, dun kynyn oll warbarth eghan, govy!

'Kemer ha gor e ynter dyns
Eghan! Govy!
An margh, may hallo cafos gwyns!'
Eghan! Govy!
Y wrek a-whethas avel gof,
Heb unwyth crya, 'Squythys of!'
Ogh, tru, dun kynyn oll warbarth eghan, govy!

Ena, ha hy ow-cones freth,
Eghan! Govy!
yn-meth hy gour, 'Na-worta! Wheth!
Eghan! Govy!
Rag namnygen yth agoras
Del dybyaf-vy, y dheulagas!'
Ogh, tru, dun kynyn oll warbarth eghan, govy!

Whath, mothow aga ober oll,
Eghan! Govy!
An whetha ufer eth dhe goll;
Eghan! Govy!
Y'n pras eskern an margh a-dryk,
Mes bryny re-wruk gol a'y gyk.

When the man saw the accident, *Alas! Woe is me!* he cried, 'It has passed out, without a doubt!' *Alas! Woe is me!* and burnt feathers in front of its nose and whispered some charm in its ear. *O pity, let us come and all sing together, alas! Woe is me!*

But it was blind and deaf, its head, *Alas! Woe is me!* it could not rise, or writhe, *Alas! Woe is me!* and then the man thought, pondering deeply, 'Hunger would not kill it!' *O pity, let us come and all sing together, alas! Woe is me!*

'Work would not kill it, unhappiness would not kill it, *Alas! Woe is me!* but for lack of breath it is dead' *Alas! Woe is me!* He called to his wife, 'Bring me your bellows!' *O pity, let us come and all sing together, alas! Woe is me!*

'Take and put it between the teeth, *Alas! Woe is me!* of the horse, so that it can get wind!' *Alas! Woe is me!* His wife blew like a smith, without once crying 'I'm tired!' *O pity, let us come and all sing together, alas! Woe is me!*

Then, while she worked quickly, *Alas! Woe is me!* her husband said, 'Don't wait! Blow!' *Alas! Woe is me!* Because, I do believe, its eyes almost opened,' *O pity, let us come and all sing together, alas! Woe is me!*

And yet all their work was a failure, *Alas! Woe is me!* and their profitless blowing was wasted; *Alas! Woe is me!* the bones of the horse remain in the field, but crows have made a feast of its flesh. *O pity, let us come and all sing together, alas! Woe is me!*

Ogh, tru, dun kynyn oll warbarth eghan, govy!

Yndella, avello, kefrys,
    Eghan! Govy!
Y'tremenna gordhyans an bys;
    Eghan! Govy!
Ha pan ve'n margh tremenys glan,
Y-res gul deweth agan can.
    Ogh, tru, dun kynyn oll warbarth eghan, govy!

An Edhen Huder

Y-teth noswyth dhe dharras agan chy
Den coth, yndelma a-wruk cows dhen-ny:

Ha my ow quandra down yn cos,
A-ughaf vy y clewys tros;
Y-clewys can un edhen tek
A-gana ton o marthus whek.
Mar whek o can an edhen-na,
Dre hus may whruk dhem hunrosa;
Yn-dan un wedhen may cuskys
Nans-yu ny-won pygemmys prys.
Mar whek o avel son es gwres
Gans gover kelys yn-dan skes;
Mar whek o avel wherthyn whar
A vyrgh ow flattra maw a-s-car;
Mar whek o, tenna mes may whruk
A'm corf ow enef, hag a-n-duk
Yn pellder, dres myl vor ha tyr,
Dre gosow du, ryp lynnow glas,
War veneth ughel, gun ha pras;
Dres hallow ledan, rosow mur,
Whath byth ny-dawa-hy nep-ur;
Dres towan, ha carrek, streth ha pol,
Ha whath y cana pup-ur-oll.
Dew! whecca gan o an gan-na,
A-wruk dhem ankevy pup tra,
Ma na-m-be prederow nahen,
Nag own Dew, na kerensa den! —
Yth-hevelly dhemmo ow bos
Mes hanter ur gensy ow-mos
Dewedha erna wruk hy han,
Cammen namoy ny-s-clewys man,
Ha'm enef arta a-dheth tre

In the same way as it, also, *Alas! Woe is me!* all the glory of the world would pass as well; *Alas! Woe is me!* and as the horse is completely gone, my song must be ended. *O pity, let us come and all sing together, alas! Woe is me!*

The Magical Bird

An old man came to the door of our house one night, and spoke to us like this:

While I was wandering deep in the wood, I heard a sound above my head; I heard the song of some beautiful bird singing a tune which was remarkably sweet. So sweet was the song of that bird that it made me dream; I slept beneath a tree, I do not know for how long. So sweet was it, like the gentle laughter of a girl bewitching one who loves her; so sweet was it that it drew my soul out of my body, and took it far, across a thousand seas and lands, through black woods, by blue lakes, on high mountains, on down and meadow; over broad heaths and great plains, but still it never fell silent; it went over dune, rock, stream and pool, and still it sung ceaselessly. God! so pleasant was that song which made me forget everything, that I had no other thoughts, nor fear of God, nor love of man! It appeared to me that I had only gone with it for half an hour till it finished its song, and my soul came home again to find its former

Rak cafos y berghen a-ve.
Mes yn le den yowynk a'y os,
Y'm cafas ena, coth ha los,
Hep nerth rak sevel ewn a'm saf,
Kerdhes hep lorgh ma na-allaf.
Ny-welaf coweth-vyth yn-few,
Ha chy ow thas ken re a-bew;
My ny-m-bus trygva yn-dan nef,
Na map na myrgh a-wor ow lef.
Mar codhes, lavar dhem pyth eth
An edhen-na dhemmo a-dheth,
Ha ladra dyworthyf dre gan
Ow yowynkneth ha'm densys glan?
Hy re-ladras, ha kyk ha gos,
Na gasa man dhem saw hunros.

Y-tewys; ena, gyllys lusow los
A-wel dhen, gans an gwyns ef eth y'n nos.

An Dullores

Hedhyu vyttyn pan sevys y-tuth sket y'm brys –
    'My a-wel ow herensa kens nos!'
Scant na-yllyn omfrona ow-cortos an prys,
    Gwyn ow bys, may-m-be cumyas dhe vos.

Pup whel-oll genef gwres, ha devedhys an ur,
    Yn ow dyllas De-Sul – nyns-o ken –
Awos bos an forth-eglos dhe'm whans kerth re hyr,
    Dres ke, sur, my a-lammas toth-men.

My pan dhuth nes dh'y darras, y-n-gwelys deges,
    Yn-dan alwheth o, denvyth y'n chy,
Rag dhe'n fer gans gwas aral hy o gyllys mes,
    Ow-cul ges an fol a-s-cara hy.

Yn nos haneth, ha tewolgow y'n pow oll a-dro,
    Gweth es tewolgow yu codhys y'm brys,
Pan brederaf, 'Namoy nyns-us gesys dhymmo,
    War nep torn tam kerensa y'n bys!'

possession. But instead of a man in his youth it found me there old and grey, without strength to stand up straight, and others own my father's house; I have no dwelling under heaven, and there is neither man nor woman who knows my voice. If you know, tell me where that bird went that came to me and deprived me of my youth and my pure manhood through a song. It has stolen both flesh and blood leaving me with only a dream.

He fell silent; then, having gone like grey ashes from our sight, he went with the wind into the night.

The Deceitful Girl

When I got up this morning, this came to my mind – 'I shall see my love before night.' I could scarcely restrain myself until the time when I should have the blessed good fortune to go.

The hour had come and the work completed, and I in my Sunday clothes – nothing else for it – and as the church road was too long a journey for my liking, for sure, I jumped over a hedge.

When I came near to her door, I saw it closed, locked fast, without anyone in the house, because she had gone to the fair with another fellow, mocking the fool who loved her.

The night, with darkness all over the country around, worse than darkness has fallen on my mind, when I think, 'There is not a single bit of love left me in the world any more!'

An Vowes Doth

Ha my owth-helghya glew
  My a-gafas
Mowes melen hy blew,
  Glas hy lagas.

Ha'n vowes a gana,
  Ena y'n ros,
Gans lef mar whek esa,
  Nes may whruk mos.

Govyn a-wruk orty,
  Tek ha dyblans,
Bay a ry dhymmo-vy
  Rag ow arghans.

'Byth na-rof' yn-meth hy,
  'Bay rag arghans:
'Rag travyth gwraf y ry
  Pan y-m-be whans.'

'Ow horf ny-beryllaf
  War an gwels glas:
War bluf py usyon scaf
  Gwell ve an cas!!'

The Wise Girl

While I was boldly hunting, I found a fair-haired girl with blue eyes.

And the girl sang, there on the heath, with such a sweet voice that I drew near to her.

I asked her, fair and square, to give me a kiss for money.

'I shall never give,' said she, 'a kiss for money: I shall give it for nothing, when I want to.'

'I will not risk my body on the grass: it would be better on feathers or light chaff!'

R. St V. Allin-Collins (Hal Wyn) 1878–19??

Hal Wyn

Whethlow, teg aga eghen,
a-s-guthel my a-ven
Rag gordhya moy an yeth wyn,
kenth-yu gorholeth pur dyn
fest garow ha marthus yen,
      Tavas fundya
      Sur ha grondya
      War seyl creffa
      Whans dhem ema.
Drefen ow bos corf hep par
Aswonves gans lues den
Ow hanow en gwyr hep mar
Yu Hal Wyn gwas Vur Vreten.
Nans-yu ugans cansvledhen
O kewses 'gan tavas len –
Prag ny vya na moy len?

Moren a'n Pow

Moren dek o, pupprys pur lowenek,
Bras hy holon, nyns-ens morethek,
hy a drygas na-pell a Lymeryk.
Rak den py benen vyth nyns-o ownek,
Hag un jeth y-fynnas mos dhe'n dre vur
Rak perna traow ha hy pennek pur.
Y-teth dhe stall mayth-o puptra ynno.
Yn-meth-hy, 'Otta le vyth da dhemmo.'
Stall bras o, mur y les, nyns-o y bar.
Manegow a-n-jeva, lyves hep mar.
Du melen, gwyn, kemyskys aga lyu,
Myns may halles-sy mennas bos yn fu!
Yn ran an stall, mayth-o'n gwara gwerthes,
Gwas tek yth-esa, an purra bugel,
Nag-o y whans mas plekya dhe gares.
An torn, pan deffa, yth-esa huvel.
Y-teth yn-rak dhe gewsel dhe'n voren.
Yn-meth ef, mur y giufter, hep powes,
'Moren whek, pandra wraf war nep cor dhes?
Parys yth-of-vy puprys dhe'th wheres!'

66

Hal Wyn

I shall tell may beautiful stories for the greater glory of the fair tongue, and although it is a very difficult task, very tiring and wondrous hard, I want to establish the language securely and set it on a stronger foundation. As I am a fellow without peer and well-known to many, my name indeed is Hal Wyn, man of Great Britain. For twenty centuries our language was spoken – why should it no longer be strong?

A Maid from the Country

A pretty maid she was, always very happy and bold and never downcast, she lived not far from Limerick. She was not afraid of man or woman, and one day she wanted to go to town, and she was very determined. She came to a stall which had everything on it. She said, 'Here is a place that will suit me.' It was a big stall and very diverting, there was nothing like it. It had gloves, and many of them. Black, yellow, white and multi-coloured, as many as you could wish on view! In part of the stall, where the goods were sold, there was a handsome fellow, quite a lad, who wanted nothing better than to please a girl. When the chance came, he was very humble. He came forward to speak to the maid. Said he very kindly, and straight away, 'Sweet maid, what can I

Govyn yn-lowenek, myns may kerry.
Y-n- gorthebys an voren, yn-fery,
'Res yu manegow dhem, ny-vern an prys.
Dysqua traow es plegadow dhe lys!'
Hag ytho, an gwas fel, y forth hep kel,
Y-whoras cals gwara hag ef ysel,
Tew ha tanow, deu ha deu, yn cosel
Derygthy a-gresa bos pur ughel.
Hy a-vyras, mur hy goth, orth puptra,
Ha cafos try far yn-mesk an gwella.
'Py gemmys arghans a-dal bos res dhes?'
Yn-meth hy tek na'n gwara kemeres.
'Bay, moy genes mar pe gwell, rak dha les.
Da yu, y-whra mam ow thas, hep mar, do
Dhe'th perna gans bayow haneth dhe nos,
Ow-ry dhes an prys a-deleth cafos.'
Hag ena hy eth mes, ughel hy fen,
Gesys an gwas avel marghak dyslen.

do for you? I am ever ready to be of ser-
vice. Happily, whatever you like.' The
maid answered him merrily, 'I need
gloves, and the price doesn't matter.
Show me some that are fit for court.'
And he, the cunning fellow quite openly
piled up a heap of goods, thick and thin,
pair by pair, in front of her until it was
high. She looked with great haughtiness
at everything and found three pairs
among the best. 'How much for these?'
she said sweetly and took the goods.
'One kiss, if you please, or more if you'd
prefer.' 'Very well, my father's mother
will come to pay you with kisses tonight
for sure, and give you the right price.'
And she went away, her head high, and
left the fellow like a faithless knight.

D.R. Evans (Gwas Cadock) 188?–197?

An Vorvran

Ass yu uskes dha hens erbyn an gwyns,
Pyscajor hep par,
Gans muvyans lun 'drelyans;
Lemmyn war enep, ena yn downder,
Omdroghyth, omdregyth,
Ha pupprys hep squythder,
Dha lergh dre an ebren 'vel seth totta tennys
Pan na vo dha gorf gans dowr an nos cudhys.
Yn cowethas an cregyn tryger an clegrow
Ty 'orryth dha nyth yn goscotter an alsyow.
Pell a anedhow mapden ha'y vur-strevyans
Yn ledander an morrow nefra hep megyans.

Enef Car

Avel menestrouthy clewys war an dowr cosel,
Avel an gwyth-pyn pan dremen an awel,
Avel an perlys yn goles an mor ow-colowy,
Avel lyes steren yn ebren a-ugh ow-terlentry,
Avel Mys Metheven ha sawor rosennow,
Avel an gluth glew ha whek erder an vorow,
'Vel splander an howl owth amma dhe'n mullyon,
'Vel tosow a owrlyn glan war an ysennow
'Vel notys an volgh los a gan yn coswygow
Avel an goverow le may tyf an tek melyon,
Avel an camneves ow' camma'n glas nevow,
Avel an commolow yn Gwlas Hus ha Pystry,
'Vel lywyow gans tekter us owth omgemysky,
Avel kekemmys hag anella anal a lander,
    Dhe'n re-na yma yn kerensa hev'lepter,
    Gwaregow pur vur, meyn-cof marthus ha tourow,
    Goskejwyth lowr a blek ha tek efan lysow:
    Ha puptra 'wra pup onen – dhe les oll yth yu.
    Mes ober po powesva a gotho dyworth nef,
    Pyu yu neb a-s-mak oll? An tyak yu ef.

D.R. Evans (Gwas Cadock) 188?–197?

The Cormorant

How swift you travel against the wind, fish-
erman without equal, full of movement and
turning; now on the surface, then in the
depth, you dive and plunge, constantly and
untiring. Your path through the sky is like
an arrow shot quickly, when your body is
not covered by the water of the night. In the
fellowship of the shells, crag-dweller, you
put your nest in the shelter of the cliffs. Far
from the dwellings of mankind and his
great striving in the expanse of the seas,
forever without sustenance.

The Soul of a Friend

Like music heard on the quiet waters, like pine
trees when the wind passes by, like the pearls
shining at the bottom of the sea, like many
stars glittering in the sky above, like the month
of June and the scent of roses, like the translu-
cent dew and the sweet freshness of the early
morning, like the brightness of the sun kissing
the violets, like clusters of bright silk on the
ears of corn, like the notes of the blackbird that
sings in the forests, like the streams where the
lovely buttercups grow, like the rainbow curv-
ing through the blue heavens, like the clouds in
the Land of Enchantment and Magic, like
colours which are blending themselves with
beauty, like everything which breathes a breath
of purity, to these there is in love a likeness to
very great arches, wonderful monuments and
towers, pleasant sheltering trees and fair broad
courts: each one does his work for the good of
all. If work and rest come from heaven, who
keeps everything going? It is the farmer.

W.C.D. Watson (Tyrvap) 188?–1959

My a Glew

My glewaf an tonnow war drethow ow frappia,
My glewaf an awel war eithin ow whetha,
My glewaf an edhyn war vagas ow cana,
Mes tavas côth Kernow ny glewaf vy henna.

Dha yêth a Vro Gernow yu drôg gans dha flehas,
Ny garons y gerryow 'ga thassow dhe glewas,
Ma drôg gans dha gevyon an deth ma dho weles,
Mes ol 'gan lowender yu whath yn dha weras.

Pa gwell gans an Sawson vel sôn aga levyow?
Na sconyeugh an Geltyon hag ol aga gerryow!
Gwreugh cara 'gas tavas en termen termennow
Ha gwedhen an Gernow gwra lesa hy delkyow.

Carol Kelinen Sans Day

Ma gron war'n Gelinen, 'ga lyu y lethwyn,
Ha Jesu 've mayles en dillas owrlyn –
Ha Mam o ha Maghteth, Marya, Mam Dew,
Ha gwedhen a'n gwella an Gelinen yu.
Kelin! Kelin!
Ha gwedhen a'n gwella an Gelinen yu.

Ma gron war'n Gelinen, 'ga lyu y gwelswer,
Ha Jesu 've crowses: E Vam en awher –
Ha Mam o ha Maghteth, Marya, Mam Dew,
Ha gwedhen a'n gwella an Gelinen yu.
Kelin! Kelin!
Ha gwedhen a'n gwella an Gelinen yu.

Ma gron war'n Gelinen, 'ga lyu y gosruth,
Ha Jesu 'gan Selwyas; enno yu 'gan fyth –
Ha Mam o ha Maghteth, Marya, Mam Dew,
Ha gwedhen a'n gwella an Gelinen yu.
Kelin! Kelin!
Ha gwedhen a'n gwella an Gelinen yu.

I Hear

I hear the waves striking on beaches, I hear the breeze blowing on furze, I hear the birds sing on a bush, but the ancient language of Cornwall, that I do not hear.

Your children, Land of Cornwall, are not fond of your language, they do not love to hear the words of their fathers, it does not please those who love you to see you thus, but all our joy is in helping you.

What do the Saxons like better than the sound of their voices? Do not refuse the Celts and all their words! Love your language for ever and ever, and the tree of Cornwall will spread its leaves.

The Sans Day Carol[1]

There are berries on the holly tree, their colour milk-white, and Jesus was wrapped in silk clothes. *And Mother was she and Maiden, Mary mother of God, and the best tree is the holly tree. Holly! Holly! And the best tree is the holly tree.*

There are berries on the holly tree, their colour grass-green, and Jesus was crucified; His Mother in sorrow. *And Mother was she and Maiden, Mary mother of God, and the best tree is the holly tree. Holly! Holly! And the best tree is the holly tree.*

There are berries on the holly tree, their colour blood-red, and Jesus is our Saviour; in Him is our faith. *And Mother was she and Maiden, Mary mother of God, and the best tree is the holly tree. Holly! Holly! And the best tree is the holly tree.*

Ma gron war'n Gelinen, 'ga lyu y glowdhu,
Ha Jesu 've marow; dredho ny a vew.
Ha Mam o ha Maghteth, Marya, Mam Dew,
Ha gwedhen a'n gwella an Gelinen yu.
Kelin! Kelin!
Ha gwedhen a'n gwella an Gelinen yu.

Covyon Keltek

Duthen war'n Un Men Scryvys – ow-cordhya,
Ha genen lyes skes:
Duthens, war newl nyjys,
Orth Bro Ancow devedhys.

Men cof VITAL TORRICI – FILIUS:
Y ven yu genen-ny –
Py le yth-esa y jy? –
Ha pan veth a-bew y bry?

Men cof Arludhes kernow —– CUNAIDE
Arlodhes vras an vro:
Cosel ynter an fosow,
Ha *motors* ow-mos yn tro.

Try yn Castel an Dynas – ow cusca:
Cof dedhyow tremenys,
Lyes cas vur wharfedhys,
Hedhyu ystor ankevys.

Dhe Vreten Vyghan dres mor – yn Ryek
Ethen-ny, war hyr for',
Dhe wlas lowenek hy dor;
Duthen pup den hy harer.

Esen-ny war Bentewn – yn Kembry:
Colon wyr pup-onen,
Gans Gorseth Berth, pur lowen,
Ny a-wruk dos dhe'n Kelgh Men.

An Orseth Breten cuntellys – yn Kernow:
Lyes Kelt devedhys,
Warlergh govyn o cowsys,
Garmow cref 'wruk son y'n bys.

There are berries on the holly tree, their colour coal-black, and Jesus was dead; through him we are alive. *And Mother was she and Maiden, Mary mother of God, and the best tree is the holly tree. Holly! Holly! And the best tree is the holly tree.*

Celtic Memories

We came praising onto the down of the Men Scrifa[2] and many a shade with us: they came, flying on mist, from the Land of Death.

The memorial stone of VITAL SON OF TORRIC;[3] his stone we have – where is his house? And what grave has his clay?

The memorial stone of the Lady of Cornwall, CUNAIDE,[4] great lady of the country: quiet between the walls, with motorcars winding their way round.

Three sleeping in Castle an Dinas: memory of days gone by, after many a great battle, history today forgotten.

To Rieg in Brittany over the sea we went, on a long journey, to a country whose earth was joyful; every one of us came to love it.

We were on Pentwyn in Wales: true-hearted every one, together with the Gorseth of Bards, very joyfully we came to the Stone Circle.

The Gorseth of Britain was convoked in Cornwall: there came many a Celt, there was speaking after asking, strong cries were sounded in the world.

A.S.D. Smith (Caradar)1883–1950

Henry Jenner

A'n Dasserghyans Kernewek ef o tas,
Mur y gerensa dhe Gernow y wlas,
Py fen-ny, na-ve ef ha'y weres bras?

Down o y skyans, cuf y golon hel,
Rak les Kernowyon mar a-ve y whel,
Gony pan ve tremeneys a'gan gwel.

Gwas Myghal a-wruk gonys has a-sef
Genen-ny, ow tevy yn gwedhen gref,
Hy gwrydhyow war an bys, hy fen yn nef.

An Gwlascarer

Ny-allaf-vy kewsel Kernewek,
Ny-allaf-vy scryfa na-whath,
Re gales yu tavas mar uthek,
Predery anodho a'm lath!

Na-gows dhem a hynwyn tylleryow,
Tevys kynth-of war an tyr,
Na lavar ow bosa-vy Kernow,
Ow devedhyans Keltek ny'm dur!

Pyth a-dal traow a'n par-ma?
An Tavas ny-vern dhymmo-vy!
Un slogan a-garaf-vy garma,
Ha 'Kernow bys vyken' yu hy!

A.S.D. Smith (Caradar) 1883–1950

Henry Jenner

To the Cornish Revival he was a father, great his
love for Cornwall his country; where would we be,
were it not for him and his great help?

Deep was his knowledge, kind his generous heart,
great was his work for the good of the Cornish peo-
ple, woe to us when he passed from our sight.

Servant of Michael[1] planted seed which rises with
us, growing into a strong tree, its roots on the
world, its head in heaven.

The Patriot

I cannot speak Cornish, I cannot write
it either, too hard is such a terrible
language, thinking about it kills me!

Do not speak to me of place names,
although I was brought up in the
country, do not say I am a
Cornishman, I care nothing for my
Celtic origin.

What worth is there in things of that
sort? I have no interest in the lan-
guage! One slogan I love to shout,
and that is 'Cornwall for ever!'

An Mytyn Warlergh

Ha my ow-cusca yn-town
Y-teth bom war an darras:
Dystough kemerys gans own
Dyfuna my a vynnas.

Hanter clewys nebonen
Ow-leveryl 'naw ur yu';
Glos trom a settyas dalghen
Ynnof – owt! ellas! ha tru!

Ha keppar ha lughesen
Y'whruk an govynnadow –
Py le? Prag? Pyu? Pyth esen? –
Deghesy war'm cowsesow.

An gorthyp ewn dhe'n re-na
Ny-wodhyen, kyn fen cregys:
Ha scon y-codhys arta
Yn cusk down, pur venygys.

Ysolt Ow-Tos dhe Gernow

Try gorhel tek yth esa kens
A settyas mes war aga hens
 A 'Werdhon bys yn Kernow:
Ow mos yth esens scaf ha cref,
Pup gol ales, ha'n gwyns adref
 Ow plegya aga gwernow.

Try alargh gwyn, gorholyon hus,
Rak lowenhe colonnoww tus,
 Ha gwres gans pystryoryon
Y halses crysy mayth ens-y,
Mar dek ha compes o an try,
 Del lever dhyn drolloryon.

An revajoryon yn deu rew
A gana lyes chanty bew,
 Ow revya yn un whesa;
Ryb pub scoth yth o costen owr
Rak surhe na dheffa dowr
 Aberveth ow teghesa.

The Morning After

I was sleeping deeply when
there came a knocking on the
door: at once I was taken by
fear and I willed myself awake.

I half-heard someone saying
'It's nine o'clock': an unexpect-
ed pang gripped me – oh! woe!
alas!

And like a bolt of lightning the
questions – Where? Why?
Who? What was I? – struck my
mind.

I did not know the right answer
to those questions, were I to be
hanged: and quickly I fell again
into a deep, very blessed sleep.

Isolt Coming to Cornwall

There were once three fair ships
which set out on their journey from
Ireland to Cornwall: they were going
swiftly and strongly, every sail out-
stretched, and the wind behind bend-
ing the masts.

Three white swans, ships of enchant-
ment, to gladden the hearts of men,
you could believe they were made by
magicians, so beautiful and skilfully
made were they, as story-tellers tell
us.

The rowers in two rows sang many
lively sea shanties, rowing and sweat-
ing; by every shoulder there was a
golden shield, to make sure that the
water did not rush in.

Res o porres fystyna mur
Has scaffa gallens hedhes tyr
    An myghtern MARK a GERNOW:
Hag ef ow cortos dres an dowr
Y YSOLT, arlodhesow flowr
    A lynyeth hen myghternow.

Ysolt whek, jentyl hy fara,
Orth hy gweles pyu na's cara?
    A 'Werdhon flowr hy hynsa:
Grasys hy form ha'y fas, del goth,
Dyghtys gans yeghes ugans bloth:
    Hy servya pyu na vynsa?

Ha hy, yn cadar war an flur
Esedhys o, ha Trystan sur
    A's gwelas pur vorethek:
Rak cuth a's teva, dew yn test,
Hy golok o prederys fest,
    Hag yn meth hy morethek:

'Govy pan esys Ywerdhon ger,
Ha'n bewnans esa hep awher,
    Ha'w mam, ha'm kescowetha!
Byth moy ny glewaf ylow whek,
Nanyl an delyn dhym a blek
    Na'n gwary-myr nowetha.'

Ena y sevys towl a wyns
Mayth o creghellys aga dyns,
    Ha'n gorghel ow lafurya:
Trystan a omsettyas yn snell
Dhe denna raf gans oll y nell
    Hedra ve'n gwyns ow turya.

Bronwen an vaghteth o pur glaf
Rak hy a's teva lyes whaf
    A'n mor, worth y dremena:
Wosa an mor dhe spavenhe
Ha nerth an corwyns dhe lehe
    Y cuscas awos henna.

Mam Ysolt o myghternes fel,
Ha gensy skyans down a'n del
    May whrelly marthys dewas:
Dewas kerensa hy a wruk
Ha'y ry dhe Vronwen, nep a'n duk
    Ma'n rolla dhe'n dheu bryas.

It was necessary to make great haste and reach as soon as possible the land of King MARK of CORNWALL: and he waiting over the water for his ISOLT, most excellent lady of the lineage of ancient kings.

Gentle Isolt, noble her bearing, who seeing her would not love her? Of Ireland she was the fairest of her sex: graceful her form and face, who seeing her would not want to serve her?

As she was in a chair on the deck, Tristan saw that she was full of sorrow: because she was regretful, may God bear witness, her appearance was very anxious, and she said longingly:

'Woe is me that I left Ireland, and the life which was without tedium, and my mother, and my companions! Never again shall I hear sweet music, or the harp which pleases me, or the latest drama?'

Then there rose a gust of wind so that their teeth were shaken, and the ship made headway slowly: Tristan quickly set about pulling an oar with all his strength while the wind lasted.

Bronwen the maid was very poorly because she had got many a jolt from the sea while travelling over it: but after the sea quietened and the strength of the whirlwind lessened, she slept.

Isolt's mother was a cunning queen, who had a deep knowledge of herbs so that she made a wondrous drink: a love potion she made, and gave it to Bronwen who bore it with her in order to give it to the couple.

Kevryn ny wodhya Ysolt man
O henna, namoy whath Trystan,
   Ha dhodho yth o seghes:
Yn-meth-ef orth Ysolt: 'Plema
Ten whek dhe eva y'n le-ma
   Rag agan les hag yeghes?'

Kettoth ha'n ger hep namoy cows
Kerghys an costrel mes a bows
   Yn kerghyn Bronwen tennys:
An gwyn yth efsons aga deu,
Hag yntredha, er aga gew,
   Kerensa a ve genys.

Trystan, hag Ysolt ryb y scoth,
Ow tos dhe'n tyr yth esens toth,
   Tyntajel tek y'n pellder:
Mark, ha ganso bryntyn ha keth,
Orth aga gortos war an treth,
   Dyghtys gans lun ryelder.

An myghtern Mark ny wodhya whath
Bos hager tenkys owth omlath
   Prest erbyn y lowena:
Us trystys moy war an norvys
Es kerensa a-vo storvys?
   Ny won: res yu gorfenna.

An Dasserghyans Kernewek

Mars osta den a Gernow
   A garro y wlas del goth,
Ny-'fyth marth a glewes barth
   Ow-cana dhe'n Tavas Coth:
Ha ty mar keryth Ystory,
Y-keryth whethel genef-vy.

Kembry yu gwlas an bronyon:
   Kernow yu gwlas an als:
Gonyow hen ha whelyow sten
   Ha pyscajoryon pals.
An yl a-n-jeves tavas bew:
Tavas y gyla marow yu.

That was a secret Isolt knew nothing about, nor Tristan either, and he was thirsty: he said to Isolt: 'Where is there a pleasant draft in this place for the good of our health?';

As soon as the word was uttered without any more ado, the bottle was brought out of the dress that Bronwen had taken off: they both of them drank the wine, and love was born between them.

Tristan, with Isolt by his shoulder, was coming quickly to the land, and fair Tintagel in the distance. Mark, with noble and servant beside him, was waiting on the beach, all adorned in splendour.

King Mark did not yet know that awful fate was endlessly struggling against his happiness: is there a greater sadness on earth than unrequited love? I do not know: it is necessary to finish.

The Cornish Revival

If you are a man of Cornwall who loves his country as is fitting, you will not be at all surprised to hear a poet singing to the Old Language: and if you love History, you will love a story by me.

Wales is the land of the hills: Cornwall is the land of the cliff: old moors and tin workings and many fishermen. The one has a living language: the language of the other is dead.

Gallas hy gober gensy,
    An wlas re-gollas hy yeth:
Tam ha tam, ass-yu drok lam
    Dhe'n Sawson yma hy keth!
Hy thus, del hevel, yu pys da
A squychya arghans map an pla.

Sawsnek yu Kernow lemmyn:
    Dysykans yu kettep flogh:
A'y bow ny-wor tra war nep cor:
    Henna a-wra colon trogh.
A wlaskerensa nyns-us tam
Yn mester, mestres, tas na mam.

Kepar ha splander myttyn
    Avar y'n jeth pan darth,
Nep golow hell ow-tos a-bell
    Yu gwelys gans an barth:
Ow-fetha an tewolgow tew
Hag orth-y-dreghy ynter deu.

Y-sevys Henry Jenner
    Ha scryva lyver fur,
Ha Morton Nance a'n sewyas gans
    Lyvrow a-dal dhyn mur.
Py fen-ny hep an dsycans da
Re-ros an dheu dhen skentyl-ma?

Mes lyvrow aga-honen
    Nyns-esens lowr dhe'n whel:
Kepar ha seth an dheu dhen eth
    Ha pregoth an awayl.
Dhe lyes tre y-tethons toth,
Dhe lyes chy ha castel coth.

'Gwlas Keltek, sur, yu Kernow,
    Ha Keltyon-oll on-ny;
Kernowyon wyw hedra ven bew
    Bedhen,' o aga cry:
'Dre wytha tavas coth an wlas
Gwren gwytha ynweth agan gnas.'

Cowethasow Kernow Goth
    O kensa frut an mevyans:
A gemmys whel ysyly lel
    Pup-oll a-n-jeves prevyans.
'Res yu cuntell ann brewyon-oll,
Na-vo gesys travyth dhe goll.'

It is all up for her, the land has lost her language: bit by bit, alas, she is enslaved by the Saxons. Her people, it appears, are willing to grasp the son-of-the-plague's money.

Anglicised is Cornwall now: ignorant is every child: about his country he knows nothing at all: that is heart-breaking. Of patriotism there is none in master, mistress, father or mother.

Like the brightness of morning when it breaks early in the day, some slow dawdling light is seen coming from afar by the poet: overcoming the thick darkness and cutting it in two.

Henry Jenner arose and wrote a learned book, and Morton Nance followed him with books of great worth to us. Where would we be without the good learning that these two learned men have given?

But books themselves were not enough for the work: like an arrow the two men went and preached the gospel. To many towns they came swiftly, to many houses and old castles.

'A Celtic country, for sure, is Cornwall, and Celts are we all; let us be worthy Cornishmen as long as we live,' was their cry: 'through keeping the old language of the land let us also keep our personality.'

Old Cornwall Societies were the first fruit of the movement: for every faithful member participated in the great task. 'All the fragments must be gathered, so that nothing is lost.'

Avel cres may hallo byrth
    Omguntell warbarth ynno,
Nyns-us le gwell, ogas na pell,
    Es del yu Gorseth Kernow.
Y'n tyller sans-ma, del dhegoth,
Offysyal yu an Tavas Coth.

Nans yu nebes bledhynnow
    Nyns-esa y'gan oryon
A-wodhya dek ger Kernewek
    Mes nebes dyscajoryon.
Lyther byth ny-vynnens scryfa:
Kewsel ny-brederens nefra.

Ass-yu ken an dedhyow-ma!
    Yn despyt oll dhe'n Sawsnek
Awotta lu ow-quytha'n-few
    An tavas coth Kernewek:
Y ny-s-teves own a'y usya,
Ow-keskewsel ha kescryfa.

A nyns-us genen Gonys
    Oll y'gan tavas tek?
Pyth yu a-n-led? Pyth yu a-n-sped?
    Mes 'Tyr ha Tavas' whek.
Yndella, Kescowetha,
    Kemereugh colon! Prak?
Kyn fo mar hell, gans mur a nell
    An mevyans a war-rak!
Ow-quytha tavas coth an wlas
Na-varwo nefra agan gnas

As a centre so that the bards can assemble together in it, there is no better place, near or far, than the Gorseth of Cornwall. In this holy place, as is fitting, the Old Language is official.

A few years ago there was no one within our borders who knew ten words of Cornish apart from some teachers. They would not write a letter: they never thought of speaking.

How different are these days! Despite the English language there are a number of people keeping the old Cornish language alive: they have no fear of using it, when conversing and corresponding.

Do we not have a Service entirely in our beautiful old language? What maintains it? What promotes it, but dear Tyr ha Tavas?[2] Therefore, comrades, take heart! Why? Although it is slow, the movement will continue with much strength! It will preserve the old language of our country so that our personality will not die.

L.R. Moir (Car Albanek) 1890–1983

An Map Dyworth an Yst

Pen an Vyaj

An gorhel dres an mor a wolyas
Wor tu ha'n Cleth gans lyes marner len
Dyworth an Yst, a dan an howl ha gwyns,
Dhe Gernow goth ha tewl rak prena sten.

Yth esa ena deudhen, an yl coth,
Y gyla yowynk, ewnter rych ha'y noy,
Ha'n meppyk Jesu henwys lun a varth,
A waytyas an deweth moy ha moy.

Gwythoryon an Eglos

An Eglos

An eglos coth a sef yn splan
Yn mysk an chyow tewl ha glas;
Hy thour a serth wor tu ha'n nef,
Ow lordya ha'n dre ha'n pras.

Dres lyes bledhen dynyver
An clogh re sonas cler ha cref.
'Deugh omma oll may perthough cof
A Dhew! Golsoweugh orth ow lef!'

Hedhyw, warlergh bledhynnow hyr,
Y perth hy lyes nam termyn;
Whath stowt yth yu yn henys clor
-- A greft dha yn tyogel syn.

Ha pyu a wruk drehevel oll
An eglos ma yn Kernow bell?
Gwren redya ha dysquedhes prest
An bobel sempel, da ha fel.

L.R. Moir (Car Albanek) 1890–1983

The Boy from the East

The End of the Journey

The ship sailed over the seas towards the North with many trusty sailors from the East, under the sun and the wind, to old and dark Cornwall in order to buy tin.

There were two there, one old[1] and the other young, a rich uncle and his nephew and the little boy was called Jesus and was full of amazement, longing more and more for the end of the journey.

The Guardians of the Church

The Church

The old church stands gloriously amongst the dark and blue houses; its tower stretches up towards the heavens, lording it over the town and the field.

Through many numberless years the bell has rung clearly and loudly. 'Come here all of you to remember God. Listen to my voice.'

Today, after long years, time has left many blemishes on it; yet it keeps its form in gentle old age – a sign of good workmanship, for sure.

And who built the whole of this church in far Cornwall? Let us read and willingly show the people, simple, good and skilled.

Gwythoryon an Eglos

Spyrysyon an Vengledhyoryon

Mengledhyoryon yth en
 Ow conys pell y'n bans;
Y treghyn men whel cref ha gwyw
 Parys rak 'n eglos sans.

Trawythyow rew a serthy tyn
 Moy menough glaw ha newl;
Whath bytegens dywysyk en
 Herwyth an myster-rewl.

Gans ewnder o an veyn degys
 Dhe'n splat yn cres an dre,
Py le may sevy pur yn ta
 An eglos war hy bre.

Ha kettep men pysadow o,
 Dustuny troha Dew
– Dhe obereth tus servabyl
 Covath pupprys yn few.

Y whortens y y'n gorflan las
 Ow splanna harth y'n howl
Bys may dewedhys cowal be
 An tour ha'n eglos towl.

Whethel an Cor Kernewek [esrann]

A, redyoryon ancoth,
Cor of hep par yn Kernow bell;
Y hallaf kerdhes saf yn dan
Colon an margh a'm mester fell.

Nebonen fur a'm gelwys Mark;
Yn certan hager merkys en
Pan entrys vy dhe'n bys ma yeyn;
Omdhevas dystough ha hep eghen.

Ken ver ow lythyow, aneth yu
Bos bras ha pos ynweth ow fen,
–– Re vras, a dyp an medhek na

The Guardians of the Church

The Spirits of the Quarrymen

Quarrymen were we, working far
out on the hillock; we cut stone
to work skilfully and worthily pre-
pared for the holy church.

Sometimes frost froze hard, more
often there was rain and fog; and
yet we were industrious accord-
ing to the rule of our craft.

The stones were carried directly
to the site in the middle of the
town, where the church stood
firmly on its hill.

And every stone was a prayer, a
testimony to God of the work of
industrious people, a memorial
for ever.

They waited in the graveyard
shining confidently in the sun
until the tower and the dark
church were completely built.

The Tale of the Cornish Dwarf [extract]

O Unknown readers, I am a unique
dwarf in far Cornwall; I can walk
upright under the belly of my cruel
master's horse.

Someone wise called me Mark; cer-
tainly I had been marked unsightly
when I came into this cold world, at
once an orphan and without kin.

Although my limbs are short, it is
remarkable that my head is so large,
and heavy too – too big, according to

Nep agan plu a rewl yn tyen.

Hebask yth of pan gothons tyn
An bommyn nes gans envy trus,
Whath my a wor ow bos moy fur
Es ow thormentors, yn ow brus.

Ow mester fell! Ogh! My a'n cas;
Den yu dhe wyr hep cufter man,
Nep lyes costyk dhym a re
Hep reson war ow thyn efan.

Myreugh! an kethwas dyllys yu;
Namoy a m cronk ow mester cas.
Na fella my a woneth prest
Ragth —yth esof pell a ves.

An Gwary-Myr [esrann]

A! Ass' o gay an wary va!
    An kelgh bras lun a dus;
Banerow splan a lyes lyw
    Ow tekhe oll an bys.

Hag ena gorhel Noy a dheth,
    Tennys gans nyver bras,
Un lester ryal, gwres a bren,
    Gans chy a warth 'hes.

'A! Myr ow thas, A! Myr ow mam,
Awotta lemmyn Noy ha'y wrek!
Yn aga herghyn lyes flogh,
Kepar hag eleth yu, mar dek.

'Ha lyes, lyes eneval
Ow tos yn sevur, deu ha deu,
Avan an blynken tyra wan
Bys mayth entrons dhe'n argh yn rew.

    'An olyfansas cref,
    Gansa lewpartas bryth,
    Ynweth an lewas fel
    Ha'n tygras, war ow fyth.
    Gostyth y eth y'n chy,
    Deu ha deu defry.

the doctor who rules the whole parish.

I am docile when the blows fall painfully on me, driven by perverse hatred, yet I know in my own mind that I am wiser than my persecutors.

My cruel master! Oh, how I hate him; he is truly a man without any kindness at all, giving me many a stripe without cause on my broad backside.

Look! The slave has been freed; my cruel master no longer beats me – I shall never again work for him – I am far away.

The Miracle Play [extract]

Oh! How pleasant was the miracle play! The great circle was full of people; flags of many colours adorned the whole world.

And then came Noah's ship, pulled by a great number, a royal vessel of wood, with a house on it.

'Oh! Look, my father! Look, my mother! Here are Noah and his wife! About them are many children, so beautiful!'

'And many, many animals coming cautiously, two by two up the weak gangplank till they come into the ark.'

The strong elephants, and spotted leopards with them, also the cruel lions and the tigers, by my faith. They went

Cun ha cathas scaf,
Mergh jolyf, a brys,
Conynas pur ownek
Ha lewern kekefrys.
Pup oll eth y'n chy,
Deu ha deu defry.'

An darras bras deges yu prest;
    Averveth, den ha best
A waytyas an nessa chons
    Dhe'n dus 'ma anes fest.

'Ha lemmyn, tus,' yn meth an Lef,
'Dres deugans deth ha deugans nos
An glaw a godhas pos hep let
Na strech; an bys yn whyr o plos.'

'Hag oll a ves cowlvudhys o
Un droklam bras war oll an bys.
An dyal ma rak tus penscaf
Profusys o hyr solabrys.'

'Dhe ves an golom a s dysqueth
Bos segh an dor; hag oll a gerth
Adar, pur certan lowenhes,
Rak daskemeres aga nerth.'

proudly in, two by two indeed. Dogs and swift cats, sprightly horses, in time, very timid rabbits and also foxes. Every one went in, two by two, indeed.'

The great door is kept shut; inside, man and beast waited for the first opportunity, very hard for these people.

'And now, people,' said the Voice, 'for forty days and forty nights the rain fell heavily without delay or rest, the world was indeed unclean.'

'And everything outside was completely drowned, a great disaster over the whole world. This vengeance on frivolous people had already been prophesied for a long time.'

'The dove shows that the earth outside is dry; and everyone walks out, safely rejoicing, to repossess their strength.'

Robert Victor Walling (Scryfer an Mor) 1890 – 1976

War Lerch an Bresel

Gwel yu'n broniou heb an huelbren
  Gwel y'un awel heb an gwez,
Gwel es clowans cledh po'n omladh
  Yu coseleth en an lez.
Gwrenz an costennow a tewder
  A uch da gregi war an gwâl,
Bedhes gortos cledh en e wain,
  Tawes e dhur rudh ha dâl.

Robert Victor Walling (Scryfer an Mor) 1890 – 1976

After the War

Better are the hills without the
beacon, better is the wind without
the cry, better than hearing sword
or fighting is quietness in the
court. Let the thick shields be
hung above on the wall, let the
sword remain in its sheath, let its
red and blind steel fall silent.

Edwin Chirgwin (Map Melyn) 1892–1960

Avon Rejerrah

An avon Rejerrah a bonyas dhe'n mor,
Sygerans yma pan dhe hell mes a dhor;
Whel-bal coth yma pan dhallethas hy res
Hag yn hy herghyn nyns us travyth saw cres.

Hep anneth an bans yu, ha gwyls yu an le,
Namenough ny dhe den-vyth oll bys y'n vre.
Redenek an keynans, kewnyek pup men,
An keynres ow frosa ha pellhe un gan.

Calmynsy yma pan dhe scaf dh'Ellenglaze,
An rajel yu gyllys derowek hep pras;
Whek yu an le-ma hag a bren y bons yn,
Moy ledan an avon, gyllys an ryn.

Y whelyr an gerghyth ha dowrgy an fel,
Pup onen anedha pyscajor smat, snell
Ow colyas pupprys pan vo sylly ha truth
Ow slynkya erbyn an gover hep uth.

Y te kendefryon dre veler ha when,
Pur uskys an avon a slynk orth y ben;
Yma galow an gulla ha lef an mor bras
Ha kelly y vewnans yn dowrow down, glas.

Y whruk tyrya omma Sen Gubert an da
Fundya y honen y lok magata;
Y tryk whath y hanow yn Fenten ha Gol
Yn kever an Gryjyans y'n blu-ma a sol.

Dhe Hanternos[1]

Y-clewys-vy tros Ancow, cannas dew
Nyhewer, pan ve cres war oll an bys.
Y-teth y dros mar bryva war y forth!
Mar pyen-vy yn cusk, ny-alsen-vy
A son an myghtern-na dhe glewes man.
Ryb tan ow-merwel my o gylles pell
A-hes an forth a-hembronk dhe'n tyr whek,
Pow-hunros, lun a govyon a gen deth.

Edwin Chirgwin (Map Melyn) 1892–1960

The Rejerrah River[2]

The River Rejerrah ran to the sea, at first oozing reluctantly from the earth; there is an old mine working where it set out on its course and there is only peace all around.

The heights are uninhabited, and wild is the place, and scarcely anyone comes to that hill; ferns grow all over the gorge and moss on every stone, and the gushing torrent moves away with a song.

All is tranquil when it comes soon to Ellanglaze, where the scree is covered with oaks and there is no meadow; pleasant is this place with its narrow wooden bridge, the river broadening and the mystery gone.

The heron and fierce otter are seen, both of them tough, swift fishermen always watching as the eels or trout slither upstream without fear.

At the confluence are watercress and weeds, and the river slides quickly to its end; where there is the call of the gull and the voice of the sea, and it loses its life in the deep, blue waters.

Here landed Saint Cubert[3] the good, and founded a cell for himself; his name endures in Well and Feast Day, for the sake of the Faith in this the parish he founded.

At Midnight

I heard the foot of Death, the messenger of God, last night when there was peace over the world. So secretly he came walking! Had I been asleep, I could not have heard a single sound of that king's. By a dying fire I had travelled a long way towards that gentle country, the land of dreams, full of the

Adref ow hadar ef o yn y saf
Kens es bos godhvos genef-vy yn-whyr
Y vos yn agan chy po ogas dy;
Mes oll an ayr o gyllys yen hep nam
Ha hem a-wruk ow gelwel mes a gusk.
Yth-esa whath kerensa yn y fas.
Hag orth-y-vyras genef nyns-o own,
Yndella orto my a-gowsas harth:
'Py vynnes-ta y'n ur-ma, Spyrys du?'
Y-wharthas, hag yn-meth ef 'Ny-whylaf
Denvyth saw unsel sul a-vo fest gwyw,
Rag henna, byth na-borth own man. Yma
An gwella pur-dha yn ow gwel ha gwyth!'
Yth eth, hag ot! kens hy bos deth
O gyllys pell an gwella yn ow chy.

Dhe'n Awhesyth

Caner colonnek,
    Lef my a-gar,
Lun a gerensa,
    Caner hep par.

Cannas an ebron,
    Car lyes el,
Colon dybreder,
    Caner a-bell.

Flogh an comolow,
    Lun agas myn,
Caner cref bys yn
    Porthow nef gwyn.

Agas can myttyn
    Syn dhym a whel;
Agas lef haneth
    Pen servys lel.

Pes da yth-of-vy
    Pan dheffo nos
Cafos dha lef whek
    A nef ow tos

Gedyer ow holon
    Dhe'n tyr a-ugh,
Tryg yn ow herwyth
    Hedra vyf bew!

memories of another day. He was standing behind my chair before I realised he was in our house or near it; but all the air had gone perfectly cold and it was that which called me out of sleep. And yet, there was love in his face, and I had no fear when I looked at him and spoke boldly: 'What do you want now, black Spirit?' He laughed, and said, 'I do not seek any but the most worthy. Therefore, never fear. The best are very well, in my sight and care!' He went, and behold! before it was day, the best in my house had passed far away.'

To the Lark

Hearty singer, voice I
love, full of love,
singer without equal.

Messenger of the sky,
friend of many angels,
carefree heart, singer
from afar.

Child of the clouds,
full are your lips,
strong singer even
unto the gates of
blessed heaven.

Your morning song is a
sign to me to work;
your voice tonight the
end of faithful service.

Glad am I, when night
comes, to find your
sweet voice coming
from heaven.

Leader of my heart to
the land above, stay in
my company as long
as I live.

An Jynjy Gesys dhe Goll

My a-gews hep let, my a-gan a goll,
War ow fossow los ydhyow gwer a-dyf,
Lun a wakter of, ynnof lyes toll,
Genef bryny du powes whek a-gyf.

My a-lavar whath a'n bledhynnow pell
Pan o lun a whel pyth yu gwak yn-whyr;
Kynth of trygva taw, gwyns ha glaw a-dell
Kepar del o tellys gans tus yn-lur.

Aga spyrysyon yn-ow-mesk a-vew,
Avel kerens da y a-dryk ajy.
Tarosvan of-vy yn gwel oll yn-few,
Nyns-us mes nos mes a-guth ow notha-vy.

Gibraltar

Dynargh! Meneth Calpe a sef yn mor glas,
Pur haval lew ota ha men-lym dha gnas.

Dyworth dowrow down du y whrussys-jy dos
Pan dheth dhyn an Golow a helghyas an Nos.

Y whrussys golsowes pan dheth an Lef bras
Ow ry dhyn tyr tevy, ha mor down ha bas.

Pur varthys dha fogow gans dowrow o gwres,
Goscotter tus wyls o mur dh'aga les.

Rak pewy dha ger lyes fether re dheth,
Dre wytha dha oryon y tryk lyes beth.

Scath alyon lowr-vyth re dheth orth dha dyr,
Pur haval loskveneth ha ty serrys mur.

Dynargh! Meneth Calpe o henwys gans Tarik,
Yn dedhyow a dhe y tryk agan Carrek.

The Abandoned Engine House

I speak without hindrance, I sing of loss, green
ivy grows on my grey walls; I am full of empti-
ness, there are many holes in me, and black
crows get pleasant rest from me.

I still tell of the distant years when what is now
completely empty was once full of work; although
I am a dwelling place for silence, wind and rain
make holes in me just as men used to make holes
in the earth.

Their spirits survive within me, they dwell like
good friends within me. In the sight of the living I
am a ghost, and only night hides my nakedness.

Gibraltar

Welcome! You stand, Mount Calpe, in a blue sea, like a
lion all of limestone.

You came out of deep black waters when the Light that
drove out the Night came to us.

You listened when the great Voice came, giving to us land
for growing, and sea both deep and shallow.

Your caves were made wonderfully by waters, a shelter for
wild men and of great benefit to them.

Many conquerors have come to possess your stronghold,
and many graves remain from guarding your borders.

Enough foreign craft have come to your land, and when
you are greatly angered you become like a volcano.

Welcome! Mount Calpe was named by Tarik,
and forever our Rock will abide.

Dew Genes, a Gerenow

Dew genes, a Gernow, gwyn nefra re by;
Fynten os a nerth, nyns us par dheso-jy:
Y'n tyller mayth ellen, dres oll an nor-vys,
Kernow, dha venydhyow yu genef pupprys!

Tyr gruglan, tyr growan, men cales y gnas,
Tyr sten, cober, ha pry-gwyn mar vas,
Dha oryon yu'n ebron, a Damar ha'n mor,
Ha prest yma Arthur ow' quytha dha dhor!

Tylleryow a voreth, tylleryow a dha,
Tylleryow coth-dybyans dhen a-nowedha,
Tylleryow a whekter, tylleryow a goll,
Dew genough, a-vyth ow dewetha ger-oll.

Mebyon Kernow

A, Vebyon a Gernow dek, seveugh, dyfuneugh!
Gans colonnow growan 'gas TYR byth na-eseugh!
Pup ger agan TAVAS yn-freth daskermereugh!
Yn-lowen pup gys agan Hendasow gwytheugh!

Edmund Henry Hambly (Gwas Arthur) 189?–197?

God Be With You, Cornwall

God be with you, Cornwall, may you be blessed for ever; you are a source of strength, there is none like you, and wherever I go through the whole world, Cornwall, your mountains are ever with me.

Land of heather, land of granite, a stone of hard nature, land of tin, land of fish, and good china clay; your boundaries are the sky, the Tamar, and the sea, and still Arthur is watching your border.

Places of longing, places of goodness, places of renewing tradition for us, places of sweetness, places of loss. 'God be with you' will be my very last words.

Sons of Cornwall

O, Sons of fair Cornwall, arise, awake! With granite hearts, never abandon your LAND! Repossess quickly every word of our LANGUAGE! Joyfully keep every custom of your Forefathers!

David Watkins (Carer Brynyow) 1892–1969

Tarth an Jeth

Cuf dhym yu an termyn res eth
   Nans yu lyes bledhen hyr,
Pan o pup Kernow Kernow gwyr
   Ow cara y wlas ha'y yeth;
Kewsel a wre arlydhy dur
   Agan henyeth ger nyny,
Cows a wre arlodhesow tek
   Hy melodyes eryow hy,
Pan glewys y'n maner ha'n hel
   Cordennow tyn an delyn whek.
Ass o fyn 'ga hessenyans fel
   Orth son whegoll yeth an gan.
Ogh! wosa henna y codhas
   War an yeth trueth ahas,
An golow deth a dhyfygyas
   Arak escar gwyls dyfeth;
Omsedhy a wruk hy howl splan
   Hy hyrnos dhu a dheth.
A'n plasow ha'n lysow a vry
   An yeth a ve helghyys mes;
Arlydhy, arlodhesow bras
   A wre whystra yeth an Saws;
Ha son athves an delyn whar
   O pell gyllys mes a'n hens –
Mes clewes arta hy son kens
   Yn crow an voghosogyon;
Dasserghys yu an lyen goth
   Dre dhywysyk scolhygyon;
Ha lemmyn ny a yl redya
   Lavar agan hendasow.
Enor kefens dres oll an pow,
   Ha revrons gweryn Kernow,
Trygens war aga thavosow
   Hag y'ga holonnow ynweth,
Y whelaf gwolow cler ow tos –
   Dhe wyr, hem yu tarth an jeth.

David Watkins (Carer Brynyow) 1892–1969

The Break of Day[1]

Dear to me is the time which passed many years ago, when every Cornishman was a true Cornishman, loving his country and his language; brave lords spoke our dear ancient language, fair ladies spoke its melodious words, when were heard in the manor and the hall the taut strings of the sweet harp. How fine was their cunning harmony with the darling sound of the language of song. Alas! after that there fell a hateful calamity on the language; the light of day declined before a wild unbeatable enemy; its brilliant sun set, its black long night came, from the mansions and the courts of renown the language was hunted out, lords and great ladies whispered the language of the Saxon; and the mature tone of the gentle harp was gone far away – but its sound was heard again in the cottage of the poor; resurrected is the old literature through industrious scholars; and now we can read the words of our forefathers. Let it have honour throughout the country; and the respect of the ordinary people of Cornwall, let it abide on their tongues and in their hearts also, I see a bright light coming, in truth, this is the break of day.

Spyrys an Meneth a Lever y Gevrynyow

A'n dalleth tewl my a sevys,
dre osow hyr ankevys,
kens den dhe Gernow wheka dheth
Byth omma y fuf soladheth.

Dre nosow garow hyr an gwaf,
dre dhedhyow tesak tom an haf,
pupprys dre hun ha der anhun
bos dynas cref byth my a vyn.

Dre osow fu hag osow dhe
a ugh pup als, a ugh pup bro
y whaytyaf nefra dres an wlas
a'm tron a ugh y'n ebren las.

Golyer of ha gwythyas ker
yth esof arluth deboner,
mententour davas, myl ha den
penfenten fur pegans tus len.

Golowva splan dhe dyr ha mor
dresof whyfla gwynsow or
y fethaf an corwynsow'n nef
hag ornaf an tarennow cref.

Rewler of dyown war ow thron
yn ugheldyryow lun a son –
yn mysk comolow tew ha bryth
pesya a wraf dha regnya byth.

Nyns us yn ban whath yn nep tu
moy barthusek agesof-vy,
'th of kehaval Mont Olympus
po nebes marthys Colossus.

'Th of avel oracl Delphi
po dew a'n howldrevel a vry
ass yu uthek ow golok-vy
ny yllyr byth ow hevelly.

The Spirit of the Mountain Tells Its Secrets

I have stood from the obscure beginning, in ages long forgotten, before men came to sweet Cornwall I had already been here many a day.

Through the long rough nights of the winter, through the sultry hot days of the summer, through sleep and sleeplessness, I will always be a strong citadel.

Through ages past and ages to come, above every cliff, above every district, I watch for ever over the land, with my peak aloft in the blue sky.

A watcher am I and a beloved guardian, I am a gracious lord, keeper of sheep, beast and man, wise source of maintenance for trusty folk.

A bright beacon for land and sea, cold winds gusting over me, I overcome the whirlwinds of the heaven, and control the strong thunders.

A fearless ruler am I on my throne in highlands filled with sound – amongst thick and grey clouds, I continue to reign for ever.

There is not aloft anywhere anything more wondrous than me, I am like Mount Olympus or the wonder of Colossus.

I am like the Oracle of Delphi or a majestic god of the East, so terrible is my appearance that it does not bear comparison.

Wilfred Bennetto (Abransek) 1902–1994

Bedwyr, po an Balores Dhewetha

Py le yma'n myghtern?
Mes de omna 'th esa;
War an als-ma y sefsyn
Ha dyvya dhe'n pray.
Mes ef re wruk fya
Pell, re bell a dre.

Y fynnaf nyja dhe'n fogo
May fe ef gesys
Y'n jeth a ve genys.
Dre an cober a'y do
My a byk rak y hedhy
Adhan Dyntajel
May whruk Mewrlyn y dhry
A ugh bys dhe'n castel
Dhe rewlya'gan bro.

Mar nyns usy ena
Muscok my a vyn
Nyja dhe'n fogevyow
Sen Agnes rag pyga
Mes an sten a-dhan ryn,
Palores an palor.
agan myghtern martesen
Ow whylas marregyon
'yl bos kellys yn pol-sten,
Encledhyes yndanno
Yn yffarnow cuth for'.

Mar nyns usy ena
Y fynnaf pyskessa
Y'n mor yntra Syllan
Ha'gan Pen an Wlas,
Ow kelwel ow Arthur,
Na vo kellys, ellas
Na vyth Kernow namur.

Saw unsel my a sef a
Baloresow'n pow ma,
Enef Kernow whath oma.
Res yu dhymmo cafos
Ow arluth kens mos

Wilfred Bennetto (Abransek) 1902–1994

Bedivere, or the Last Chough

Where is the king? Only
yesterday he was here; on
this cliff we stood and
dived on our prey. The king,
where is he? But he has
fled far, too far from home.

I will fly to the cave where
he was left the day he was
born. Through the copper
of his roof I will peck to
reach him from under
Tintagel, where Merlin
brought him up into the
castle, to rule our land.

If he is not there, I will fly
madly to the caves of Saint
Agnes to peck tin out of its
hiding place, a chough for a
digger. Our king, perhaps
could have got lost in the
tin mine looking for
knights, and been buried
under it in the road of
secret hells.

If he is not there, then I will
fish in the sea between
Scilly and our Land's End,
calling my Arthur so that he
be not lost. Alas, that
Cornwall will be no more!

I alone remain of the
choughs of this land, the
soul of Cornwall I am still. I
must find my lord before he
leaves us forever, to free the
Celtic throat from the grasp
of English fingers.

Dyworthyn bys vyken
Rak frya a'n dalghen
An besyas Sawsnek
War vryansen Geltek.

Agan rychys otena!
My a byk dre an sten,
Dre an pry, dre an cober
Men-growen ha'n leghen.
My a dhyf, yn ow ober,
Gans harth pyscajoryon
War an bryly ha'n hern
Daskemeres an pythow,
May ferwys Kernowyon.

Doro dhym pryas
May tasvewo chogha
Warbarth yn cowethas
Kens de mernans dhe'm ran
May tassorghys vyth Kernow
Ha Calespulgh whath cledhya!
A ny'm gweres den vyth?
Doro dhym pryas
A Ywerdhon, Kembry!
Ny res dhe'n balores
Merwel. Sylweugh an bry,
An enef agan gwlas!
A ugh an als wyls
Y fyn nyja y'n ayr,
Hyrethek ow honen
Erna vydhaf vy budhys,
A gonfort, my tewys,
Ena Kernow hep er.

Behold our wealth! I shall peck through tin, through clay, through copper, granite and slate. I shall dive, at my work, with gallant fishermen onto mackerel and pilchards, repossess the mines where Cornishmen died.

Give me a spouse so that a chough may rise again, a companion to me before death comes, so that Cornwall may be resurrected and Excalibur flourished again. Will no one help me?

Give me a spouse, O Ireland and Wales! There is no need for the chough to die out. Save the honour and soul of our country! Above the wild cliff I will fly through the air, longingly by myself till I am drowned, with only a scrap of comfort, and I having fallen silent, and Cornwall then without an heir.

Margaret Pollard (Arlodhes Ywerdhon) 1903–1996

Gwersyow

Ny wrussys ow maga, ny wreta ow hara,
Altrewan os dhymmo, ny gowsaf dha davas,
Ny-th-tur my dhe vewa, ny-th-tur my dhe verwel,
Whath moy my a-th-car ages golow ow lagas.

Lyn gay dhys y-whyaf, hag owrlyn y-whraf,
Y-tekhaf dha drygva, y-tyghtyaf dha vara,
Dha fas mar pyth lowen, os mar dek avel eleth,
Ass-of-vy pys da ... assa-wraf-vy dha gara!

Myrgh alyon y-fydhaf y'n chy-ma bys vyken,
Ny-wreta ow hasa, ny-wreta ow hara.
Ny-th-tur my dhe vewa, ny-th-tur my dhe verwel,
What moy my a-th-car ages golow ow lagas.

Arlodhes Ywerdhon [esrann]

Ty Gernow yu henwys gwlas
Marthus tek an howlsedhas
Rych avel Myghternes vras
Dre gober, sten, ha puscas,
Nefra na ve map alyon
Genes-sy degemerys
A Gernow, yeyn dha golon,
Kens y vos genes ledhys.

Lyes den y tyswrussys
Gans dha alsyow hep mercy:
Gans den ty a vyth traytys
Ha gwerthys dre falsury.
Ty Kernow a vyth dyswres
Dre dha vebyon, als ha treth:
Ty a gyll tekter ha cres,
Ty a gyll lyen ha yeth.

Pella na sergh orth an meyn,
Ty Arlodhes Ywerdhon!
Nyns us nerth y'n besyas yeyn,

Margaret Pollard (Arlodhes Ywerdhon) 1903–1996

Verses

You did not rear me, you do not love me, you are a stepmother to me, I do not speak your language, you do not care whether I live or die, and yet I love you more than the quick of my eye.

Beautiful linen I shall weave for you, and make silk, decorate your home, and prepare your bread, if your face, as beautiful as angels, be joyful, how happy I am … how I love you!

An alien's daughter I shall be in this house for ever, you do not hate me, you do not love me, you do not care whether I live or die, and yet I love you more than the quick of my eye.

The Lady of Ireland [extract]

You are called, Cornwall, the wonderfully rich land of the West, rich like a great Queen with copper, fish and tin; you never welcomed strangers, cold-hearted Cornwall, before you killed them.

Many a man you destroyed with your merciless cliffs: by man you will be betrayed and sold through treachery. You will be destroyed, Cornwall, cliff and beach, by your sons: you will lose beauty and peace, you will lose literature and language.

Cling no longer to the stones, you Lady of Ireland! There is no strength in the cold fingers, there is no warmth in the heart.

Nyns us tomder y'n golon.
Whath kepar ha ros puscas
Bagas ster byhan a sef:
Cotthes a vyth dha olyas
Hag y ow sevel y'n nef.

Steren yu lagas tarow
A wolow y'n howldrevel;
Wosa termyn cot, hep wow,
Steren ger a wra sevel:
Pup tekter oll re gerys,
Pup tekter oll us hep nam,
Y'n steren yu cuntellys
Ruthvelen avel tanflam.

Yn mys Me, termyn Gwaynten,
Wosa ty dhe vos marow,
Avellos kettep rosen
Y'n lowarth a dhek blejyow,
Ha pan dheffo Gwaf, del won,
Ty steren ruth a dhassergh
Avel rosen y'n ebren
Pan vo ros oll yn-dan ergh.

Yet a little constellation will rise like a fish net: your watch will be cut short when it rises in the heavens.

A star gleams like the eye of a bull in the West; after a short time, for sure, a beloved star will rise, every beauty I have lost, every beauty which is without stain, in the star they have been gathered, orange like a flame.

In May, during the Spring, after you die, like you every rose in the garden will bear flowers, and when Winter comes, as I know, you the red star will rise, like a rose in the sky when all the heath is under snow.

E.G.R Hooper (Talek) 1906–1998

A Pena Prydyth

Bones y'm gallos
pygemmys a rossen
ryma ha gwersya,
ry an bys y whrussen.

Owth omlath orth geryow
ha gans gramer omdowl
an awen a fyll dhym
-yma kellys ow thowl.

Dhe gana heb astel
ewn kepar hag edhen
yn freth ow leverel
bones barth a callen.

Pluven y kemeraf
ha paper arygthy
mes nyns af war rak
ha tewlel a wraf vy.

Mebyon Kernow

Mebyon a Gernow, ny, omsevel gwren,
   Yn mes an escar pellheen,
Lyver hag arader, geseugh y
   MYGHAL AN GOF a's gelow why.
   Myghal an Gof a'n gelow-ny hogen,
   A Vebyon Kernow, ny omsevel gwren!

Mebyon a Gernow, byth na vedheugh lows,
   Yn sol, ytho, erbyn an Saws,
Kenyn del en-ny canow agan bro,
   'Kernow bys vyken!' pynag vo.
   Myghal an Gof a'n gelow-ny hogen,
   A Vebyon Kernow, ny omsevel gwren!

E.G.R.Hooper (Talek) 1906–1998

If I Were a Poet

If it were in my power,
how much would I give
to rhyme and to versify,
I would give the world.

Fighting with words
and wrestling with
grammar, my muse
fails me, and my pur-
pose is lost.

If only I could sing
without breaking off, as
sure as a bird, to speak
fluently and be a poet!

I shall take a pen, with
paper by it, I shall not
go on but I shall fall
silent.

Sons of Cornwall

Sons of Cornwall, let us arise, let us
drive the enemy far away, leave book
and plough, MICHAEL THE SMITH[1] is
calling you! *But Michael the Smith is
calling us, sons of Cornwall, let us
arise!*

Sons of Cornwall, do not ever be negli-
gent, rise up against the Saxon; we will
sing as we go along songs of our coun-
try, 'Cornwall for ever' wherever it may
be. *But Michael the Smith is calling
us, sons of Cornwall, let us arise!*

[Pup Comolen]

Pup comolen a'steves glaw
  Ow tremena avan
Ha pup eythynen war an hal
  'Ma dhedhy hy blejan.
Ny res dhyn palas a der dro
  Na teyla nyns yu res,
Y-flejow melen eythyn whath,
  Kerensa prest a bes.

Oll y'n vledhen nyns us seson
  Ha glaw ha gwyns po rew
Dres hager awel eythynen
  Yn owr pan gwyskys yu,
Dres ergh ow tysquedhes hy lyw,
  Metheven avel flam,
Hag avelly-hy, kerensa
Pupprys yu noweth-flam.

Yn nos Gwaf ogas dhe'n tan
  Omgara ny a wra;
Gwaynten a dhe ow ton blejyow
  Hag ynweth kerensa;
Manalow Kynyaf pan dewlyn
  Y-tryg kerensa sur
Pan goth an del dyworth an gwyth
  Us genen hag a dhur.

[Every Cloud]

Every cloud passing above has
rain, every furze bush on the
moors has its flower. We do
not have to dig around or
spread fertiliser, the yellow
furze will still bloom, love lasts
for ever.

Throughout the year there is
no season when the furze
bush is not dressed in gold, be
there rain or wind or stormy
weather. It shows its colour
over the snow, in June it is like
a flame, and like it, love is
ever brand-new.

On a Winter's night near the
fire we love each other, Spring
comes bringing flowers and
also love; when we cast the
sheaves of Autumn, love
abides, when the leaves fall
from the trees, it is with us
and endures.

E.E. Morton Nance (Gwas Gwethnok) 1909–

An Brythen Kernewek

Crows GWYN Sen Peran clos a dhro
Dhe'n Baner Rythsys DU mamvro,
   Ha'n Brythen braf a Gernow!

Y whyskyn Plegen OWR ha DU;
Lyw scos Myghterneth Kernow yu,
   Gans besons aga Hernow.

Palores DHU a nyj aa ugh
Atlantek GLAS, 'gans gelvyn COUGH:
   Ot! Awen Arthur Kernow

E.E. Morton Nance (Gwas Gwethnok)1909–

The Cornish Tartan

The WHITE Cross of Saint Piran brings praise
to the BLACK Freedom Banner of the
Motherland, and the fine Tartan of Cornwall.

We wear a kilt of GOLD and BLACK: it is the
colour of the shield of the Kings of Cornwall,
with the bezants of their Cornwall.

A BLACK chough flies above the BLUE
Atlantic, with a RED beak: behold the inspi-
ration of Cornwall's Arthur.

Hilda Ivall (Morvran) 1910–

Peder Can Ver: II

Y clewaf prest trosow an dre
Ow-tarenna lent dhe'n nef,
Darrasow kerry tan a-gronk;
Yma whath dha lef.

Y whelaf lemmyn chyow men,
Chymblys, mur a gochys bras,
Caunsys cales, forth legh-veyn;
Yma whath dha fas.

Y-trygaf-vy 'mysk pobel guf.
Yma dhym cowetha vas.
Yma wharth an fleghes vyghan.
Ydhyn a-gan a-ugh an pras;
Yma whath dha ras.

Nebes Gwersyow: I

Plema'n gan a wren-vy cana
Nans yu bledhen, scaf hy thros?
Pan dheth y'n jethtarth son an ydhyn
Owth-yskynna dres an buthyn,
Y ros an howl yn ro y dhos.
Plema'n gan a wren-vy cana?

Plema'n bardhonek a-wrussta scryfa
Nans yu lyes bledhen hyr?
Pup lavar tyn a'm muvyas,
Gwyr y styr adro dhe'm cumyas.
Y porthaf whath ow thrystys mur.
Plema'n bardhonek a-wrusta scryfa?

Plema'n cres re-wrussyn kelly
Dres bewnans bysy? Plema'n cres?
Yma an bobel ow-stevy, ow fysky,
Nyns us termyn predery po dysky;
Tybyans yu chassyes scon dhe ves.
Plema'n cres re-wrussyn kelly?

Hilda Ivall (Morvran) 1910–

Four Short Songs: II

I hear the sound of the town thundering slowly to the heavens. Car doors slam, there is still your voice.

I see now houses of stone, chimneys, many large vehicles, hard pavements, a paved way; there is still your face.

I live among kind people. I have good friends. There is the laughing of little children. Birds sing above the meadow; there is still your grace.

Some Poems: I

Where is the song I was singing a light-footed year ago? When there came in the dawn the round of the birds rising over the meadow, the sun gave its coming as a gift. Where is the song I was singing?

Where is the poem you wrote many long years ago? Every concise sentence moved me, true its meaning about my farewell. I still bear my great sadness. Where is the poem you wrote?

Where is the peace we have lost through busy lives? Where is the peace? The people are hurrying and rushing, there is no time to think and learn; thought is quickly driven away. Where is the peace that we have lost?

Plema ow bewnans ber yu gyllys
Kepar del eth an seth y'n nef?
Yma an bardhonogow ha'n canow
Ow-tescryfa mur a'y rannow.
Nyns yu lowr an cana freth-ma;
Nyns yu lowr.
Mes aberth yn cosoleth efan an brys
Yma pup tra prest dasvewys.

Nebes Gwersyow: II

Prak y teugh-why dhym yn nos hep fyn
Pell mes a dermyn res eth, covyon tyn?

An Flogh
An flogh ow-crenna, wonek ha dyslyw,
Y'n nos a-gryas, pan wolowys tan
An jyn-nyja y'n nef ow-tywy fell.
Y codhas yn-mysk tros an stryf ha bell.
Yth esa gonnys mur ow-tenna ughel
ha lenwel 'n ebren efan a byn cruel.
An chy a-godhas. Go-ef! Bys an flogh
O kellys oll yn-tyen y'n droklam tewl.

An Car
Prag y whren-ny dathla freth hep fyn
Adro dhe stuth an bys ha brys an dus?
Ena ny a whylas ewna'n bys
Dre dornys da ha geryow lun a vrus,
Dre nerth an scryf yu creffa whath es arf.
Y'n ur ma medhek os, attes dha fara,
Yn pow estren. Cowlwres nyns yu dha vrys
Menystra del wruk Schweitzer der y gana.

Car Aral
Prag y tressys-sy dhym cara len
A brofas ganso pup lowena oll?
Y kerys-vy den aral. Ken y fya
Ow fara mar ragwellen-vy dha goll.
Ow howeth ker, yth esta ledhys fell.
Dha vernans yeyn o costyans pos an bell.

An Caradow
Prag y fynsys-sy dyswul kerensa
Ha gensy an gallos lywa, mur y brys?

Where is my short life which is gone
as the arrow passed in the heavens?
The poems and the songs describe
many of its parts. This fluent singing is
not enough; it is not enough. But with-
in the capacious calm of the mind,
everything is constantly revived.

Some Poems: II

Why do you come to me endlessly in the night, out
of a time which has gone, troubling memories?

The Child
The child, trembling, fearful and pale, cried out in
the night when fire illuminated the aeroplane blaz-
ing fiercely in the heavens. It fell amidst the sound
of the strife and warfare. Big guns were firing high
and filling the broad sky with cruel pain. Woe to
him! The world of the child was utterly lost in the
dark disaster.

The Friend
Why did we debate enthusiastically and endlessly
the plight of the world and the mind of the people?
Then we sought to put the world to rights through
good deeds and words full of wisdom, through the
strength of writing which is stronger than any
weapon. Now you are a doctor, comfortable your
circumstances, in a foreign country. Though your
ambition to serve was not fulfilled – like
Schweitzer and his music.

Another Friend
Why did you bring to me faithful love offering every
joy? I loved another man. I would have behaved
differently if I had foreseen your loss. My dear
friend, you were cruelly slain. Your cold death was
the heavy price of the war.

The Beloved
Why did you want to destroy a love which had the
priceless power to colour? Did you not see the

A ny welsys-sy y'n lyes lyw ow-splanna
Tomder kerensa? Melen owrek, ruth,
Gwer, purpur, glas ha mur a lywyow erel
Kemmyskys fyn dhe wul an patron druth
O gwyys y'gan bewnans, gwyn ow bys!
Pra y whrussta-jy y gowldhystrewy?
Dha avy cuth a whylas prest dyswul
Pup preder bryntyn, orth y drelya dour
Dhe vewl, wherowder, traytury ha gyl.

Prak y teugh-why dhym yn nos hep fyn
Pell mes a dermyn res eth, covyon tyn?

Nos tewl, gas dhym ankevy oll yn-tyen
Ow thybyans squyth.
Coselha pup cof-oll yn cusca druth.

Dus, myttyn cler, yn splan an howldrehevel,
Tomha an comol gwyn; chass pell an lor,
Ha scull an golow owrek dres an mor
Pan omles an tewas glyp, dydros an treth
Leven hag efan yn golowder ryth an jeth.

Dus, bewnans noweth, dus.
Gwra ragof dalleth glan,
Del wra pup dethtarth splan.

warmth of love in the numberless glorious colours? Golden yellow, red, green, purple, blue and many other colours mixed beautifully to make a bright pattern which was woven in our life, to my great joy? Why did you completely destroy it? Your secret jealousy always tried to destroy every sublime thought, turning it stubbornly to resentment, bitterness, betrayal and deception.

Why do you come to me endlessly in the night, out of a time which has gone, troubling memories?

Dark night, let me forget completely my tired thoughts. Make every memory quiet in precious sleep.

Come, bright morning, in the shine of the sunrise, warming the white clouds; drive the moon far and scatter the golden light over the sea when the wet sand spreads out, soundless the smooth and wide beach in the free brightness of the day.

Come, new life, come. Make for me a pure beginning as does every bright dawn.

An Venen Goth

Ah, crysy a wrussons bones marow an venen goth,
Rak termyn hyr esens ow quaytya hy thremenva;
Ha kemmys a-s-tevo whans, ha kemmys gwyth, a'y thaga!
Wosteweth hy o marow, ha marow yn fas;
An venen goth hag o mar dykly gul dhedhy,
An venen hag a wruk gul dhedha crenna adherygthy.
Lemmyn yn tyogel hy o marow,
Ha nyns o nahen dhe wul
Saw unsel scullya an fekyl
Dagren bynak derak hy thus,
Ha gul dhrehevel men bras war hy horf,
May cothfo pup-oll hy-bos-hy cowl tremenys.
Mes pandr' yu hemma?
Myl wragh an jawl!
Yma-hy war hy beth arta!
Hy yowynk, lowenek, cref
Ow trettya yn dan hy threys
Yn un dons gwyls, garow,
hy vysour a venen goth ha'y queth usyes.

Tomás Mac Neacaill (Gwas Kendern) 191? – 197?

The Old Woman[1]

Ah, they believed that the old woman was dead; for a long time they had been expecting her passing; and how many wished to strangle her, and how many times! At last she was dead, and well dead; the old woman so difficult to deal with, the woman who made them shudder. And now for sure, she was dead, and there was nothing else to do but shed a cunning tear in front of her kin, and raise a great stone over her, so that every one would know that she had gone. But what is this? A thousand witches of the devil! She is out of her grave again! She is young, joyful, strong! Trampling under her feet in a wild, harsh dance, her old woman's mask and her worn out garment.

Frederick MacDowall (Map Estren Du) 191?–197?

An Gok

Edhen vras kepar ha pyasen ell
   Lyes gwyth clewes es gweles yn ta,
A Soth yn gwaynten ef a dhe yn hell,
   'An lef gwandra-ma' gans son an pyba.
Kyn fo oy cok yn myth stranj yu genys
   Prof a dhyslelder nyns usy, mes kens
A vetya 'fowt chyow' gans mur a les,
   Drok ober, soweth, mes sur yn y hens.
Dhe Est, son deublek an gok tryst pan yu
   Kepar ha del us an edhen ow fyllel,
A'n gwelyow glyp ha'n gwyth a bup tu
   Y te glaw yeyn hag awel ow tewel:
Pan yu kellys a vlejen Haf lyw ha lok,
   Ena a-hy dhe hy thre Soth, an gok.

Tanow Yowynkneth

Pan dhegeaf ow deulagas
Y whelaf tanow yowynkneth:
Tan an gof: tan an fogow bras,
Tan an bugel dre nos ha deth,
Po tansys gans mok yn lanow
Ow trelya dres gwelyow gans nerth,
Tanow ow crakkya yn keow
Serry worth gwynsow freth a Verth
Ha, dhe nos, nep prys, dhe nep pyk,
Yn flammow mur aga seth.

Magata yma tan unyk,
Usy ran vryntyn a bup oll deth,
Kepar ha bara yu po leth;
'Tan -olas' yu gylwys an tan-na,
Otta helder ynno hep meth
Confort fest tom ha lowena.

Yma joy whek owth-esedha
Arak tan-olas wosa con
Yn kelgh tylu attes mar dha,
Gwell hen yu es travyth a won.

Frederick MacDowall (Map Estren Du) 191?–197?

The Cuckoo

A large bird like a tawny magpie, which is
heard more times than seen, it comes 'that
wandering voice', with a sound like piping
slowly from the South. Although the cuckoo's
egg is laid in a strange nest it is no proof of
unfaithfulness, but a way of meeting advanta-
geously 'the housing shortage', and although it
is a bad deed, alas, it is a sure method. In
August, when the double sound of the cuckoo
is sad as if the bird were tiring, from the wet
fields and the fields all round come cold rain
and dropping wind: when colour and scent are
lost from summer flowers, then the cuckoo
goes to its southern home.

Fires of Youth

When I close my eyes I see the fires
of youth: the fire of the smith: the
great fire of the furnaces, the fire of
the shepherd night and day, a bon-
fire with tide of smoke turning with
strength over fields, fires crackling
in hedges and becoming angry with
the swift winds of March and at
night sometimes shooting up to a
point in flames.

Just as good is a single fire, which is
an excellent part of every day, as
bread or milk: 'hearth fire' it is
called, what unabashed generosity
is in it, such warm comfort and joy!

There is a sweet delight sitting com-
fortably in front of a hearth fire after
supper, a family circle, that is better
than anything I know.

Gweleugh tus arak an tan-pren,
Po myreugh orto, yn nep park,
'Tan-camp', ow tomma mebyon len
Gans frygow oll mok aga harg;
Cowetha freth yns-y gans can,
Yn golow splan a'n tansysow,
Hep wothvos y a hol yn ban
An olow hen a'ga thasow.

See people before a wood fire, or look at it in some field, 'camp fire' warming trusty lads, filling all their nostrils with smoke; they are merry friends, with a song, in the bright light of the bonfires, little realising they are following the ancient tracks of their forefathers.

Helena Charles (Maghteth Boudycca) 1911–1997

[A Varrak Ker]

A varrak ker
  Gwellha dha jer,
Ha clew ow husul vy,
  Mar mynnyth cres
  Y-fyth dhe'th les
Omry dhe'th negys tejy.

Helena Charles (Maghteth Boudycca) 1911–1997

[Dear Knight]

Dear knight, cheer up and listen to my advice; if you want peace, it would be better for you to concentrate on minding your own business.

Phoebe Procter (Morwennol) 1912–

Pyu a Wor an Den A-Garaf?

Pyu a wor an den a-garaf?
Deryvys yu dhe'n molghas-du;
Y hanow ker ken na-lavaraf
Colonnek gansa kenys yu.
   A Dhew, yn nos
   Yn ow hunros,
Danvon-ef arta dhem dydros.

My a-wel yn y dheulagas
Golow glas an stergan-oll,
Hag y lef yu tecca es
Anal whek an whybanol.
   A! dus yn-scon
   Ow huf colon
Rag confort yn govyjyon.

An tecca blejyow a-vyth terrys,
Garlont whek a rosennow,
Lylyow rag ow gwella kerys
Dyworth ros ha scorennow.
   War les an nor
   Ha ton an mor
A-garaf nefra – pyu a wor?

An Gwaynten

Awot-omma dalleth an vledhen,
   An howl tek a-span,
War bup bagas byghan ha gwedhen
     Pup edhen
      A-gan.

Yn olow an awel Gwaf tewel
   An Gwaynten a-dhe
Lowenek ow-carma yn-ughel
     Hag an newl
      A-lehe.

Phoebe Procter (Morwennol) 1912–

Who Knows the Man I Love?

Who knows the man I love?
It is known to the blackbirds:
although I do not utter his
dear name, it is sung boldly
by them. O God, send him
noiselessly again to me at
night in my dreams.

I see in his eyes the blue
light of all the starshine, and
his voice is lovelier than the
sweet breath of the flute. Ah!
come quickly, my dear heart,
for comfort in my sorrows.

The fairest flowers will be cut
for a pleasant garland of
flowers, lilies for my best
beloved from heath and
branches. Across the earth
and the wave of the sea, who
knows whom I love?

The Spring

Behold here the begin-
ning of the year, and the
beautiful sun shines, on
every little bush and tree
every bird sings.

On the heels of dark
Winter comes the Spring
joyfully and calling aloud,
and the mist lessens.

Pup map a-vyn mos gans y voren
   Gans k'rensa ha wharth,
Ow-terry del noweth a scoren
      Yn poryon
         Warbarth

Mes my a-dal kyny morethek
   Dyvres pell y'n Est,
Warlergh ow fow kerys mar uthek
      Hyrethek
            Ha tryst.

Every lad will go with his lass, with love and laughter, to pluck new leaves from a branch, together in the pastures.

But I must lament mournfully, exiled far in the East, for my land which I love so fearsomely, longingly and sadly.

Harold Edey (Peder an Mor) 1913–

An Balores (Can Warlergh Mordon)

Yn golow an howlsedhas y-whel yn hy skes;
An frappya hy eskell y a-dhasson y'n cres.
Py spyrys yu henna ow-kelwel mar wyls?
'Ma Palores Myghtern Arthur gan edhen sacrys.

'Ma marow an Balores, an Balores Kernow.
Ny-glewyn, ny-glewyn hy garmow.
An howl cough a-derlenter war wonyow an vro
Mes ena whath na-moy ny-vew hy spyrys, dh'gan go.

Pyu re-s-ladhas, pyu re-wruk gul an drokober-ma?
Sawson ha Normans a-dryghas mar dha,
A bobel agan mam-vro! Dysquedheugh 'gas goth
Bos Kernow un genethel bedhens arta 'gas both.

A-welough? An Balores re-glewas hy yeth!
Gernowyon, lowenheugh, re bo gwynvys an jeth!
An edhen a-omles hy eskelly du.
'Gan Myghtern Arthur whath marow nyns-yu.

142

Harold Edey (Peder an Mor) 1913–

The Chough (After Mordon[1])

In the light of the sunset we see its shadow; the beating of its wings echoes in the peace. What spirit is this which is calling so wild? It is the chough of King Arthur, our holy bird.

Dead is the chough, the chough of Cornwall. We hear not its wings, we hear not its cries. The red sun flashes on the downs of the country, but its spirit is no longer living there, to our sorrow.

Who has killed it, who did this evil deed? Saxon and Norman conquered so well. O people of our motherland! Show pride, let your will be for Cornwall to be a nation again.

Do you see? The chough has heard its language. Cornishmen, rejoice, blessed be the day! The chough spreads its black wings. Our King Arthur is not dead.

Margaret Norris (Brosyores) 192? –

Poldice

Cudhys yn-tyen yth os yn nans,
Ha breow adro dhys a bup tu,
Ynos bupteth y synsyn sans,
Covyon mar wyr ha gwyw
A'n dedhyow pell-na yu passyes;
Covyon hyrethek a'th sowynyans
A whel sten bryntyn pan ve gwres,
Ow ry dhe lyes den aga megyans.
Lemmyn, ellas, oll yu chanjyes,
Nyns us tra vyth-oll a sef
rag cofhe dhyn a'th vraster, mes
Cuth an whel, los, whath cref.
An keth re-na yu dha wythysy,
Bys vynary orth dha woskesy.

Margaret Norris (Brosyores) 192?–

Poldice[1]

You are completely hidden in a valley, with hills about you on every side, with everything in you that we consider sacred, memories so true and worthy of those distant days that are gone, nostalgic memories of your prosperity, when it was made from a noble tin mine, giving many men a livelihood. Now, alas, everything is changed, there is nothing standing to remind us of your greatness, but the mournfulness of the workings, grey yet still strong. These are your guardians, sheltering you forever.

Richard Gendall (Gelvynak) 1924–

Hendrez Diures

Ha me a moaze en tereath tewl an noaze,
Gwandra aleaze,
Vor vinack me reeg dewez, lowanheys,
En cuskah, me reeg kerras war an oon,
Han velwhez a cana, âh! mar wheage!
A euh an eithin teage,
Mar veare soon!
Thysompyas, confort thom sperez,
Sone an moare me a glowas,
Vel gwenz en grig a hanas,
Buz straft me a thevinas,
Hag en plynch lagas ma hendrez
Pell tha veaze o gellez,
Avêl skêz.

Nadelack Looan!

Rooz ew an voaren wellz en gea,
Gwidn ew an bern,
Glaze ew an pînbren reb an drea.
Pedn en ebbarn.
Ethan vean, che a veath tha vrowian
Ugge ve tha urra pot the vridgan.

Peder an prednier zêah ma fallia,
Lebmes e voell,
Dyckles an oon, cannes y embla,
Yein an thôl.
Ruddock whegen, che a veath da thidgan:
Gorta teken, terebah me tha voaze than gegen.

Looez ew an egliz, teage y thour,
Euhall ha creav,
An vola laze a grye y gour,
Garow y leav.
Kebar theeze tha vara, ruddock ownack,
Che a veath aweath Nadelack.

Richard Gendall (Gelvynak) 1924–

An Exile's Dream

As I went in the dark land of the
night, wandering abroad, I
chose a stony way, joyful.
Sleeping, I walked upon the
down, while the lark sang, oh!
so sweetly! above the lovely
furze, so great a blessing!
Suddenly, a joy to my spirit, the
sound of the sea I heard, like a
wind in the heather whispering,
but at once I awoke, and in the
blink of an eye my dream far
away had gone, like a shadow.

Happy Christmas!

Red is the wild berry in the hedge,
white is the hill, green is the pine
tree by the village, head in the sky.
Little bird, thou shalt have thy
crumbs after I have put a pot on to
boil.

Peter splits the dry logs, his axe
sharpened, wretched the down,
bleached her sides, cold the vale.
Robin dear, thou shalt have thy
morsel: wait a moment, while I go
to the kitchen.

Grey is the church, lovely her tower,
high and strong, the fieldfare calls
her mate, harsh her voice. Take to
thee thy bread, timid robin, thou too
shalt have a Christmas.

Perave an Gunneau

Ca! Gweetho agoz ruzza genz ago prassow pooz,
Leb ma an golam wastya y bownaz cooge en cooz,
Perave an carrigi wae an gunneau mar reeth,
Leb ma an velwhez cana, han bodnack bean brith.

Gohelas me a ra keveris an dreath han aules,
Leb ma an haviers scrawly vel kelion ploos casaus.
En porth na ellam cavaz buz lisstry sport didaul,
Than gunneau me vedn fya, ha boaze ma hunnen ul.

Edn telhar a orama ew ethick teage ha cuzal
Leb ma a tevy arran hag eiz du war an ambel,
Ha ennah seere a ellama gorwetha en louare aise,
Thom treiz tormentil melyn, thom pedn an redan glaze.

Hag ennah ma a tebry greath du an gwarrack medall,
Han devaz myen-du genz ago eanas evall;
Hag ennah ma an lûarn a treegaz dadn an bren,
Hag ennah me vedn treegaz, henrosa heb worvan.

Leesteevan

(Thort Leeds)

Pe goth an newl han hilgeth mar ahas
Tha Lesteevan an breze ve a drayle,
Teage y mena glase,
Gwêr y deel.

An Jowhall

Thera jowhall teage tha ve,
an tecka tegan oll en beaze,
meare e breeze,
metham e dy,
ha genam et a doola keethez,
gwidna drus!

Buz mar deage ova,

I Prefer the Downs

Bah! Keep your valleys with their heavy pastures, where the pigeon wastes her empty life within the wood, I prefer the rocks on the down so free, where sing the lark and the little speckled pippit.

I will shun the beach and the cliff where the holiday-makers swarm like dirty hateful flies. In the harbour I only find aimless pleasure boats, to the downs I shall flee, and be on my own.

One place I know that is mighty fine and peaceful, where grows the myrtle and whortleberries on the hill-side, and there surely I can lie in plenteous ease, at my feet the yellow tormentil, at my head the green fern.

And there pastures the black herd of sleek cattle, and the black-faced sheep with their meek lambs, and there lives the fox under the hill, and there shall I live, dreaming endlessly.

Launceston

(from Leeds)

When falls the fog and the soot so hateful, to Launceston my mind turns, fair her green hillside, verdant her leaves.

The Jewel

I had a lovely jewel, the fairest jewel in all the world, great its value, I dare swear it, and with me in my hands hidden, so fair a gemstone!

But so beautiful it was, so wonderfully beautiful, that I

mar varthis teage,
na algama omwetha
dres an cock e zensge
treeth a beaz broaze ham beaz raage,
malgama gwellhaz dresta
luhas e golan,
peccara tanow glaze itna,
thur bedgeth faulz an moare,
elyn, elyn a gollowy,
Deew! Fatel o peath a vry!

Saw, lapsipa me a vee,
ha tha gotha me an garaz,
ha tha vethy me an gwellaz,
mar thyag ha mar thowne,
than gullas lebmen gellez,
vel stearan vean pell thurtam.

Ha na ell an colan credia
drewa gellez lebma ...
gene ve e vea gwell
merwall kenz vel kelly hedna.

Soon gen Minfel

Me ra cuntell minfel feen
Mal boaze tecka whaeth a meen,
Mal boaze tubma a dew welv,
Mal boaze suttla whaeth a leav.
Sone a leav gwrenz ea boaze
Neverah vel an golowas,
Ha ma gwessyow meddal, teage,
Xarra sygan seavy wheage.

Gero vy boaze ennis en moare,
Meneth euhall war an doare,
Dreath an noaze betham stearan,
Gwellan greav than ri ew gwadn.
Ma ra browy heb falladow
Menze dean eze et an pow,
Ha na ra dean en noare
Bith a droage en neb vor.

could not stop myself from holding it over the boat between my thumb and forefinger, that I might see through it the lightning of its heart, like blue fires in it, from off the treacherous face of the sea, bright, bright glinting, God! How valuable a thing it was!

But I was careless, and I let it fall, and I saw it sink, so lazily and so deep, to the bottom now gone from me, like a little star.

And it is not possible to believe that it is gone from here ... it would have been better for me to die rather than lose it.

A Charm with Yarrow

I will pluck fine yarrow that my face may be yet more beautiful, that my two lips may be warmer, that my voice may be more seductive. May the sound of my voice forever be as the lightning, and my lips soft, beautiful, like the juice of sweet strawberries.

Let me be an island in the sea, a high mountain on land, through the night I shall be a star, a strong staff for the weak. I shall bruise without fail every man that is in the country, and no man in the world shall ever harm me in any way.

Tectar

Tectar a wellave bup tewe,
Lagagow glaze wellave, gwêr, tewl ha due,
lagagow ew lagannow war an oon,
lagagow avel pollow en polprye,
po lidnow lean a lew,
neverah wherhin,
meare rinwhethol:
gullow ens ha down avel an moare,
bold an niel turn, po dres orol cloer;
mar deage an'gye dre vadna ve
meeras vickan ort angye.

Tectar a wellave bup tewe:
bear an bleaw ha heere an bleawe a wellave;
nagew dua moya du,
nagew gwidna kalah gwidn,
neverah spladna,
neverah gwayah;
mallew genam prest e dava.

Tectar a wellave bup tewe:
rooz an gwessyow igge wor a dinia,
rooz vel kein an veuhick Thew,
rooz vel criban casack coose,
rooz vel an goose;
mowns a cowz ha whetha,
ha wherhin, ha baya,
ha gallas a holan gongans.

Tectar a wellave bup tewe:
medall an sely, heere, hyblyth,
carra skyriow an annon;
whar an doola,
cuzal an bezias;
lobm an pedn dowlen,
uz na ellama omweetha rag o gwellhaz;
devran medall dadn an bowz,
lebma vengam goerah bith a fedn
ha poaz, poaz,
poaz heb gorvan.

Beauty

Beauty I see on every side, eyes blue I see, green, dark and black, eyes that are pools on the down, eyes like pools in a claypit, or lakes full of colour, ever laughing, greatly mysterious, bright they are and deep as the sea, now bold, now modest, so beautiful are they that I wish to look for ever at them.

Beauty I see on every side: short the hair and long the hair I see, blackberries are not blacker, white straw is not whiter, ever shining, ever moving, eager am I ever to touch it.

Beauty I see on every side, red the lips that tempt me, red as the back of the lady-bird, red as the woodpecker's crest, red as blood. They speak and breathe, and laugh, and kiss, and I have lost my heart to them.

Beauty I see on every side, soft the limbs, long, supple, like the branches of the ash tree, gentle the hands, gentle the fingers; rounded the knees, so that I cannot help seeing them, soft bosom beneath the dress, where I would place my head and rest, rest, rest for ever.

Pandrama?

Pandrama?
Ha che gellez lebma,
pandrama?
Lavar them!
Fatel veath lebmen!

Rag ma glihi a toaze nevra
dres a holan,
tidn pubonen carra cletha.
Pe ra ve tibias an dra,
pandrama?

Maiteth, kerra voze,
stearen ma noaze,
che leb me a gavaz,
han oatham ve mar vroaze,
che leb me a gollaz,
ha mar ethick thosympyas,
a nakevy skân a ra che,
pell kettel vethta?

Rag me a lavar theeze,
ma holan ethew terrez,
ha che thurtam gellez!

Fatel o wheage sawarn an tabm oane!
Fatel o medall gon gwille toor!
Fatel o gwidn skelly an goolan!
Fatel o creav hudol an moare!
Han garrack looez
reeg kosgaza gon crengah,
fatel o vaze!

Ham doola aith tha vleaw owriack
pell reeg doane,
tha vleaw medall bedn ma daorn,
ennah dadn an garrack,
han tegennow urt tha scovurnow
theram o clowas prest bedn ma boh.

A verth, A floh!
Tha che pe reeg ve abma,
kellez vema,
ha kellez lebmen neverah
che a veath tha ve,

What Shall I Do?

What shall I do? Now that
thou hast gone away,
what shall I do? Tell me!
What happens now?

For icicles keep stabbing
through my heart, sharp
each one as a sword.
When I think of it, what
shall I do?

Maiden, dearest girl, star
of my night, thou whom I
found, when my need was
so great, thou whom I
lost, and so terribly sud-
denly, wilt thou soon for-
get me, as soon as thou
art far away?

For I tell thee, my heart it
is broken, now thou art
gone from me!

How sweet was the scent
of the thrift, how soft was
our turf bed, how white
were the wings of the gull,
how strong was the magic
of the sea! And the grey
rock that sheltered our
love, how useful it was!

And my hands the scent
of thy golden hair long did
bear, thy soft hair against
my hand, there below the
rock, and the jewels at
thine ears ever I feel them
against my cheek.

O maid, O child! When I
kissed thee, lost was I,
and lost now for ever thou
wilt be to me, and I do not

ha n'ora ve pandrama,
hebos che.

Cles?

Cles et agoz cader
En telhar sawe ha close,
Amisk leeaz dadder,
En skesse peder fôs,
Per ko an ri heb voza,
Ha than bownas dre veath dewa,
Ha deew ell seere requyrya
An kethe noaze ma goz ena.

A Jhesu kear caradow,
Gwraze clowas gon pedgadow,
Ha graunt tha nye tha woollo,
Rag neverah venitho.

Glawe a ra heb glibia
Tabm veeth tha whye an pedn,
Ha whye prest en omgersya,
Mar gles deraage an tane,
Buz leeaz ma gorwetha
Heb voza, tane na bara,
Na ello whye gotheffia
Tabm bean dah tha rima?

A Jhesu kear caradow,
Gwraze clowas gon pedgadow,
Gweras thene perry ko
Oatham rerol a vo.

know what I shall do,
without thee.

Comfortable?

Snug in your chair in a safe
secluded place, amidst many
good things, in the shelter of
four walls, remember those
without walls, and that to life
there will be an end, and
God may surely require this
same night your soul.

O, dear beloved Jesus, do
thou hear our prayer, and
grant us thy light for ever.

It rains without in any way
wetting your head, with you
ever making yourself at ease,
so snug before the fire, but
many lie without walls, fire
or bread; can you not vouch-
safe a little bit of goodness to
these?

O, dear beloved Jesus, do
thou hear our prayer, help us
to remember the needs of
others as may be.

Pew a Ore?

(Caon rag an kenezlow Keltek)

P'eare veath duah oll an zoer?
P'eare veath clerya an ebbarn?
P'eare vedn doaze an deeth dethewes
Pa veath duah oll than poan?
Pew a ore?
Heere an vor,
Meare an zoer adro tha nye!

Deeo, broderath, onen gwreze,
Deeo, an wherith kekeffrys,
Rag fra na vedn ny joynea?
Reall dra hedna a veea!

Pew a ore?
Heere an vor,
Meare an zoer adro tha nye!

Dewvil vlethan ew, ha mouy,
Aba reeg nye doaz dreath moare …
Genz an moare o nye debarres?
Wos an teere veath lebmen zoer?

Pew a ore?
Heere an vor,
Meare an zoer adro tha nye!

Dre vo neverah genen frothe,
Ha nye cowas mar veare zoer,
Ma gye laddra agon tirriou …
Fatel veath, than? Pew a ore?

Pew a ore?
Heere an vor,
Meare an zoer adro tha nye!

Contrevogion, deen warbar
Dres an mena, dres an moare!
Puna spladnar, puna crevdar
Nye a veath thene, pew a ore!

Pew a ore?
Heere an vor,
Meare an zoer adro tha nye!

Who Knows?

(A Song for the Celtic Nations)

When will be an end of all the anger?
When will the sky clear? When will
the promised day come when there
will be an end of all the pain?
Who can tell? Long is the road, great
is the anger around us!

Come, brothers, united, come, sis-
ters also, why will we not unite? A
wonderful thing that would be!

Who can tell? Long is the road, great
is the anger around us!

Two thousand years it is, and more,
since we came over the sea ... By the
sea are we divided? Because of the
land, will there now be anger?

Who can tell? Long is the road, great
is the anger around us!

While there is ever strife with us, and
we having so much anger, they are
stealing our lands ... What will hap-
pen, then? Who can tell?

Who can tell? Long is the road, great
is the anger around us!

Neighbours, let us come together
across the mountain, across the sea!
What glory, what strength we shall
have, who can tell?

Who can tell? Long is the road, great
is the anger around us!

Dirrians Nature

Setha itta looar pe rama,
Ha gweithaz an gwelz mar ware,
Ha clowas an ethan tha gana,
Ha ogel an bledgiow cair,
Han kennesan scurria en delkiow,
Han pagerpau serry than mean,
Aneth ew nag iggans maraw,
Mar garow ew gwewan mabdean.

An Ennis

Hunz en creis an lidn
Ema an ennis,
Dew y lomman widn,
Lebma revy pimpernel,
Luzu leath kevris,
War ketep gwarha moel.

Nangew ree goath ma gorhall,
Towlaz war an dreath,
Han dowre ree thownw ha tewal
Malgam moaze thy en feith,
Buz kebmys eze them hirrath
Rag kerras ennah whaeth!

Whela Ve

Pell en beaze a vema,
Reall, reall ma gowg,
Moare ha teere a pewy,
Leall perhen ove am oge,
Me wellaz levyaw Dava,
Tha Zillan reeg kerras trooz zeath,
En cooze Carrack Looez me reeg helly
Ors, bleath ha baeth.

Creeg ha carn ma anath,
Euhall, euhall dres an pow,
Urrian ma gulasketh

The Survival of Nature

When I sit in my garden, and
see the grass so green, and
hear the birds singing, and
smell the beautiful flowers,
with the spider scurrying in
the leaves, and the lizard
clinging to the stone, a won-
der it is they are not dead, so
harsh is the heel of mankind.

The Island

Yonder in the middle of the
lake is the island, two her
white hillocks, where grows
pimpernel, milkweed too,
on each rounded summit.

Too old is now my ship,
cast upon the beach, and
the water too deep and
dark for me to be able to go
there in confidence, but
however great is the long-
ing I have to walk there
even so!

Seek Me

Long in the world have I been,
royal, royal my blood, sea and
land owning, true one am I ever, I
saw the floods of Dava, to Scilly
did walk dry shod, in the woods
of the Mount.[1] I hunted bear, wolf
and boar.

Barrow and crag my dwelling,
high, high across the country, the
boundaries of my kingdom round
Tamar and sea. The gold of

Tamar ha moare a vrow.
Ema genam aur Worthen taves,
Padn an thihowbarth keffres,
Torch Troeth me a wellsa pure weare
Tha poonia poran bis en moare.

Lew spladn an howle genam kevez
En tullalulla an noaze,
Nag eze preze na vema gwellez
Na telhar veeth hep ooll a throoz.
Me a whethas gen mogion ha broazian
Tha Loundres pa gerras an lu,
Ha kyny gen mibbian goviggian,
Oll po tho gew.

Whela ve.

Ireland have I touched, cloth from southern parts likewise, Twrch Trwyth[2] I saw rightly running right into the sea.

The bright colour of the sun I have found in the gloom of the night, there is no time that I was not seen, nor any place without my footprint. I laughed with commoners and great when the host marched to London,[3] and mourned with the sons of sorrow, when all was grief.

Seek me.

Richard Jenkin (Map Dyvroeth) 1925 –

Pask

Pask – gwaytyans Gwaynten yu pupprys,
Dasserghyans sugan yn gwyth hag yn howl y des,
Dyfuna blejennow hag oll natur yn bys,
Ha lowender yn colon dhynny gans Pask yu dres.

Pask – gwaytyans yu a Sylwans an bys.
Dasserghyans Cryst re dhasprenas oll Mapden
Ha dyfuna enevow dhe Vewnans nefra a bys.
Lowender Nef ny ran ganz Eleth len.

Richard Jenkin (Map Dyvroeth) 1925 –

Easter

Easter – always it is the hope of spring, the renew-
al of sap in trees and warmth in the sun, awaken-
ing flowers and every natural thing. Easter brings a
joyful heart to everyone.

Easter – it is the hope of Salvation, Christ's
Resurrection has redeemed mankind and wakened
souls to everlasting life, heavenly joy we share with
angelic hosts.

Jon Mirande (An Menedhor) 1926–1972

Avar Kens Vora

Avar kens vora y-whruga sevel,
  Buf benen noweth y'n bora,
Omgwetha 'wrug gans dyllas owrlyn
  Ha'n howl yn sevys awartha.
Arlodhes y-fuf yn cres hanterdeth
  War goscar efan ow-rewlya,
Ha kefrys y-fuf gwedhowes yowynk
  An howl pan sedhas-ef arta.

'Syr Yrygaray, ow arluth kerys,
  Na seveugh yn-ban agas pen!
Boken ymava genough-why edrek
  Orth ow demedhy, martesen?'
'Nag us yn-tefry orth dha dhemedhy
  Edrek genef-vy nagonen,
Ha nefra ny'm byth edrek na moreth
  Bew war an nor-ma hedra ven.'

'Yth esa dhymmo caradow whegoll,
  Kyn whren-ny dhe'n oll y geles.
Dhe'n oll y geles a-wren, bytegens
  Dhe Dhew y'n nef o dysclosyes.
Hy a wruk danvon dhym colmen-vlejyow
  O gans flowrennow dyblans gwres;
Gans blejyow dyblans yth esa gwrugys
  Ha gwenwyn 'th esa yn hy cres!'

Synsy re wruga corf an den marow
  Dre seyth bledhen y'm stevel yn,
Aberth y'n pry yeyn hedra ve an deth,
  Y'n nos ynter ow dywvregh tyn.
Y lanhe a wren gans dowr-lymaval
  Un deth pup seythen-oll yn-dan ryn;
Un deth pup seythen-oll my a'n glanhy;
  Hen o De Gwener dhe vyttyn.

Jon Mirande (An Menedhor) 1926–1972

Early Before Morning

Early before morning I arose, I was a bride in the morning, I dressed in silken clothes, the sun having risen to its zenith. I was a lady ruling a great retinue in the peace of midday, and also I was a young widow when the sun set again.

'Sir Yrygaray, my dear lord, raise up your head. Or do you regret having married me, perhaps?' 'I do not regret having married you at all, and I shall never regret or be sorrowful while I am alive on this earth.'

'I had a beloved sweetheart, although we concealed it from everyone, from everyone we concealed it, but to God in Heaven it was revealed. She sent to me a knot of blemishless flowers; with blemishless flowers it was girded, and poison was in its centre.'

I held the dead man's body through seven years in my narrow room, in the cold clay while it was day, at night between my taut arms. I cleaned it with lemon juice one day every week secretly. One day every week I cleaned it: that was Friday morning.'

Dewheles a Wra

Dewheles a wra whath an hen wenylly
   ha cregy a'th valcony aga nyth,
gans an askel gwaryek, war y gwarels
   arta gelwel a wrons;
mes an re-hons a wruk dysky aga hynwyn,
   dewheles byth ny-wrons.

Dewheles a wra whath an gwythvos lonak
   hag yskynna '-nowyth keow an garth,
aga flourys whath tecca y'n gorthewer
     omgery a wrons.
mes an re-hons, pos gans gluth myfynen
orth y dheverennow hag y yn-cren
hag avel dagrennow an deth ow codha,
   dewheles byth ny wrons!

Dewheles a wra'n gerensa, ha dasseny
   arta y'th tywscovarn hy geryow tom;
dha golon-sy mes a dhownder hy huscas
   par hap dyfuna 'wra;
mes dylavar, transyak, war bendeulyn,
   del y-whordhyr arak Y alter Dew,
del y'th kerys-vy, na omdull ... yndella
   dha gara byth ny wrons!

They Will Return

The old swallows will return again
and hang their nest from your bal-
cony, they will call again with play-
ful wing on its panes; but those who
learnt their names, they will never
return.

The bushy honeysuckle will return
and once again climb the hedges of
the garden, its flowers will open still
lovelier in the evening; but those
heavy with dew, with drops shaking
on them like the stars of the day
falling, they will never return!

Love will return and echo its warm
words in your ears; perhaps your
heart will wake from the depth of its
sleep; but speechless on bended
knee, speechless as if worshipping
God before his altar, as I loved you,
do not deceive yourself, they will
never love you like this!

R.M. Royle (Pendenhar) 1926–

Cornel Kernow

Ro dhymmo-vy cornel yn Kernow
War veneth a ugh an mor,
Ena clewes bys vyken an tonnow
Ha cusca yn dan an ster ha'n lor.

Gor ow threys ena yn Kernow,
Kerdhes an gerthva y'n eythyn,
Ple wheth an gwyns ynter an blejyow
Hag a splan gluthennow y'n myttyn.

Enclath ow eskern yn Kernow,
Yn dan a balas whegh tros-hes
Ryp an eglos us awartha'n alsyow,
Gans an hendasow pupprys yn cres.

Delyrf ow enef yn Kernow
Plema pupteth ow tryga ow holon,
Gwandra dres cosow ha pentyryow,
Ha bewa bys vyken yn lowen.

An Edhen Dhu

Spyrys Kernow – a wrugavy dha gafos?
My re wruk dha whylas lyes bledhen,
Mes p'ur ny brederys adro dhys
My a wruk dha gafos yn cowel edhen.

My a brederas dha vos y'n alsyow,
Po orth omgeles y'n avennow.
Y fynnys dha glewes yn canow an dus,
Y'n gwyns war an gonyow hag an mordonnow.

Mes my a'th cafas hedhyu yn Deunans,
Prysner tryst yn pow estren,
Spyrys Kernow hag a gefys worteweth,
Yth o edhen whek du yn cowel edhen.

My a's gwelas drehevel hy fen,
Ha ruth hy gelvyn ha ruth hy garrow.

R.M.Royle (Pendenhar) 1926–

A Corner of Cornwall

Give me a corner in Cornwall on a
mountain above the sea, to hear there
the waves for ever, and sleep under
the stars and the moon.

Put my feet there in Cornwall, to walk
the path in the furze, where the wind
blows between the flowers and drops
of dew shine in the morning.

Bury my bones in Cornwall, digging
six feet down by the church on the
top of the cliffs, with the forefathers
forever in peace.

Release my soul in Cornwall, where
my heart abides every day, to wander
over woods and headlands, and live
joyfully for ever.

The Black Bird

Spirit of Cornwall, did I find you? I have
sought you for many years, but when I
was not thinking about you, I found
you in a bird cage.

I supposed you were on the cliffs, or
hiding in the rivers. I wished to hear
you in the songs of the people, in the
wind on the moors and the sea-waves.

But I found you today in Devon, a sad
prisoner in a foreign country. The spirit
of Cornwall I found at last, a sweet
black bird in a birdcage.

I saw it raise its head, red its beak and
red its legs. The sun shone on the

An howl a splannas war an balores,
Hag ena y kefys spyrys gwyr Kernow.

Dus Dhym

Y tutheugh dhym y'n myttyn
Gans menkek cuntellys a'n gonyow.
Why a ammas dh'ow dorn yn scaf
Gans mynyon mar glor avel gover.
Deulagas maga tewl avel kesen,
Why a whystras 'Dus dhym, ow herensa.'

Y tutheugh dhym y'n hanterdeth
Gans myllas hag ys an parcow.
Why a ammas dh'ow bregh dre dekter
Gans mynyon mar whek avel mel.
Deulagas ow splanna y'n howl,
Why a whystras 'Dus dhym, ow herensa.'

Y tutheugh dhym y'n dohajeth
Gans tegynnow dyworth an mor.
Why a ammas dh'ow honna yn cosel
Gans mynyon keppar ha del blejyow.
Deulagas lun a wrys splann
Why a whystras 'Dus dhym, ow herensa.'

Y tutheugh dhym y'n gorthewer
Gans camneves terrys a'n ebren.
Why a ammas dh'ow bogh yn-pluth
Gans mynyon tom dre wynsow haf.
Deulagas mar wolow avel gluthennow,
Why a whystras 'Dus dhym, ow herensa.'

Y tutheugh dhym dhys dyworennos,
Y'gas lufyow owr an lorgan.
Why a ammas dh'ow ganow yn-whresak
Gans mynyon ow lesky gans howlsedhas.
Deulagas gans tan gans an stergan,
Why a whystras 'Dus dhym, ow herensa.'

Y tutheugh dhym may cuskys
May tyfunys dyworth an myttyn.
Why a ammas dh'ow holon gans ambos
A gres ragof-vy bys vyken.
Hag ow enef ow splanna gans keweras,
My a whystras 'Dof dhys, ow herensa.'

chough, and I found the true spirit of Cornwall.

Come to Me

You came to me in the morning with ling from the downs. You kissed my hand lightly with lips as cool as a stream. With eyes as dark as peat, you whispered 'Come to me, my love.'

You came to me at midday with poppies and corn of the fields. Sweetly you kissed my arm with lips as sweet as honey. With eyes shining in the sun, you whispered 'Come to me, my love.'

You came to me in the afternoon with jewels from the sea. You kissed my throat quietly with lips like petals. With eyes full of bright crystal you whispered 'Come to me, my love.'

You came to me in the evening with a rainbow plucked from the sky. You kissed my cheek tenderly with lips hot from the summer winds. With eyes as light as drops of dew, you whispered 'Come to me, my love.'

You came to me at nightfall, with the gold of the starlight in your hands. You kissed my mouth warmly with lips burning with sunset. With eyes on fire with the starlight, you whispered 'Come to me, my love.'

You came to me where I slept so that I woke with the dawn. You kissed my soul with a vow of peace for me for ever. With my soul shining with fulfilment, I whispered 'I come to you, my love.'

Goulven Pennaod (Cadvan) 1928–

Gwyns ha Glaw

Siehst du im takt des strauches laub
schon zittern? --Stefan George

Gwyns ha glaw war an dor segh,
gwyns ha glaw war eneb ow gwlas,
a dhassergh cosel a'y beth?
Avel an cuscador re hunas re hyr
yma'n losow war sevel aga manallow
a lam ughel troha'n howl dew ruyf.
Glaw glan an dedhyow los ha tewl,
an las os a dhyfun an natur lafuryes,
an dhewas dhe-les a dhyseghes an ys;
ha ty, gwyns sans, ow whetha conneryak
y hesyth dhe-ves genef ow frederow anfur
ha'm ownekter a blek derak an denkys.
Re be benygys byteweth y'th froth
hag y'th vrath a wolgh an gos coth
a resa yn gwythy kenethel squyth.
De yu termyn an tewas ha'n seghes,
otta devedhys dhe-vas prys an bewnans,
bewnans an dus ha dasserghyans an poblow.
Awen a wyns a wheth a-dhyworth bar an bans,
golow an glaw a dhowr fentynyow an spyrys.
Gwyns ha glaw war enep ow gwlas.

Goulven Pennaod (Cadvan) 1928–

Wind and Rain

*Do you see the leaves of the bush already
quivering in time? –Stefan George*

Wind and rain on the dry earth, wind and
rain on the face of my country – will it rise
quietly again from its grave? Like the sleep-
er who has slumbered too long, like the
crops about to raise their sheaves towards
the sun, monarch divine. Pure rain of the
grey and dark days, you are the drink that
awakens worn nature, the beneficial liquor
which quenches the thirst of the corn; and
you, holy wind, blowing frenziedly you sow
my unwise thoughts away from me, and my
cowardice bends before fate. May you be
blessed for ever in your noise and your bite
which wash the old blood that ran in the
veins of a tired nation. Yesterday was the
time of the sand and the thirst, here is a
time for life happily come, the life of men
and the resurrection of the peoples. The
inspiration of a wind blowing from the sum-
mit, light of the rain from the water of the
springs of the spirit. Wind and rain on the
face of my country.

Donald Rawe (Scryfer Lanwednoc) 1930–

Can Os Cres

Guden an tewennow a grull ha troylla, owth omnedha
Whytheklow cornwhylen ha plentya whymbrel, gans ujow
A vorwennol ha gwylan ow raylya. Tamaryskow
A bleg hag ynclynya, y pychons ha cravas an nef.
O omma
A lemmyn ha nefra
Tyreth hyreth ow yowynksys-vy
Keynvor dygonforth a'm cofhe
Passyes ha pupprys
Ow whylas –

Whethfyans a'n mordarth a seth ha pellhe, ow kesunya
Breghow ha delyow dhe'm dahlyow an downvor
Ow tyrusca dh'an sortas kervys-na. Morbyasen
A nyj, hanter pysk, gwan an brylly vyghan.
Rak a by le
Rak mar ha menough
Ogevyow tewl dall pleth y whylys
Crygyow moyha pell le may synsys
Po ha prag
Ow pos –

An garrek codhys usy ow nyja y'n comolow, hag omguntell
Scullyon a choghys gans whelyow hanter ankevys
Odytys gorrys yn gwythy yowynk. An balores
A dhyeskyn war y legh, ow kyny agan gwlas.
Del ena,
Alemma ha nepprys
Tourow terrys a'w gorvyn
Mun crakkys a'gan yeuny
Omma hag alena
Ow cothvos –

Donald Rawe (Scryfer Lanwednoc) 1930–

Song of Middle Age

The tangle of the dunes curls and
spins, intertwining dotterel pipes
and whimbrel plaints, the scream-
ing tern and brawling kittiwake.
Tamarisks bend and bow, they
lunge and scrape the sky. Oh here,
oh now and never, yearning land-
scape of my youth, desolate
seascape of my ageing, then and
always, seeking –

The surge of surf sinks and with-
draws, combining tentacles and
fronds, my dahlias of the deep,
abrading all those fond sea-
urchins. A guillemot swims, half
fish, to spear the little mackerel.
For whence, for if and often, dark-
est caverns where I sought, far-
thest fissures where I grasped,
whether and wherefore, being –

The plunged and soaring rock is
flying in the clouds, mixing with
jackdaw trash and half-forgotten
mine works, adits driven into
youthful lodes. The chough lights
on its ledge, mourning for our race.
So then, so hence and sometime,
broken towers of my ambition,
flawed metals of our desire, here
and henceforth, knowing –

An Lowarnes

An lowarnes a scryj y'n cos
A'n deweth a'n jeth; ha dres
An avon, cosel avel gweder,
Son-ma pych, dha enef ow throllya,
Dha golon gans own ow wana.
Prag an tros a wra yndella
Dha sawthanas hag a'th huda,
Ha pup-oll nep y gweles?

Cry coth yu, dyworth a dhalleth an bys:
Cry noweth bys vyken, cry fell hag hyr,
Na vos denagha. Agan yeuny yma,
Agan gwaytyans, h'agan mur tewl.
Yma my ha ty agan honen, kerensa:
agan whylas, an yl rag y gyla:
Agan uth dhe gelly agan ena kesynsys,
Kens gallos dalleth an bewnans
Us ethom dhyn cafos worteweth.

Caradow a'm enef, fatel yma ethom
Dhym ragos: moy es dhe'n lowarn
Ethom, ethom tanek rag lowarnes…

The Vixen

The vixen screams in the wood at the close of day; and over the river, still as a mirror, the sound stabs, twisting your soul, spearing your heart with fear. Why does the sound amaze and fascinate you, and everyone who hears it?

It is an ancient cry, from the beginning of the world, a cry forever new, yet terrible and long, not to be denied. It is our desire, our hope, and our darkest fear. It is you and I ourselves, my love, searching for one another, our terror at losing our united spirit before real life can start, which we must find in the end.

Darling of my soul, how I need you: more than the fox feels desire, a burning need, for the vixen...

W. Morris (Haldreyn) 1937–

Keresyk

Keresyk, tecca es keresen -os
     Dhym nep a'th car; drefen
  Gwedhra pup bledhen gwedhen
  Saw lun a ras prest os len.

Cucow Bretonek yn Porth Kernewek

Yn dan nef splan ha havek
My a-wruk kerdhes war an fordh
A-wyus ryp an meneth.
Hag a-wra hembronk troha'n porth.

An porth gans chyow byghan
Drehevys a ven-growyn tek,
Hag a-sef ryp an arvor
A'm Kernow, tyreth braf ha whek.

Y-whelys a-dheragof
War an mor, war an dowrow bas
Ogas dhe'n cay, an cucow
A Vreten Vyghan, gwyn ha glas.

Yth-esa war bup huny
Lystry-cok melen, ruth ha gwyn;
Y'whrens gul lywyow lenter,
A-dhastewynya y'ga lyn.

An golow yth-o plegys,
Hag yth-esa pup den y'n dre,
My a-wruk aga clewes
Ow-kewsel gans ton Morlaix.

Pur ylow o an levow,
Hag yth-o dh'aga thavas coth
Sonow Keltek gothvedhys.
Y oll a-wruk y gows gans goth.

An rosow a-wre segha,
Gell y'n howl; scrawas a-wre dos

W. Morris (Haldreyn) 1937–

Little Sweetheart

Little sweetheart, fairer than a cherry
are you to me who loves you; because
although a tree withers every year you
are ever full of grace, and faithful.

Breton Boats in a Cornish Port

Under a blue and summery heaven, I
walked on the winding road by the
mountain, which leads towards the
harbour.

The little houses of the harbour were
built of beautiful granite, and it
stands by the shores of my Cornwall,
a fine and gentle land.

I saw before me, on the sea, on the
shallow waters, the white and blue
boats from Brittany, near to the quay.

On each one were yellow, red and
white floats: they shone with colours
reflected in the water.

The light was pleasing, and every
man was in the town, and I heard
them speaking with the accent of
Morlaix.

The voices were very musical, and
their ancient tongue had a familiar
Celtic sound. They all spoke it with
pride.

The nets were drying, tawny in the
sunshine; black-headed gulls were
coming to flit above, screeching with
a resonant noise.

Dhe drenyja a-wartha,
Owth-uja, heglew aga thros.

Y-cluttyens, re-anedha,
A-van war wernow, ewn ha serth;
Mes trusprenyer pryjwyth ens
Rak cucow ny-dryk pell yn perth.

Res o dhe'n cucow byghan
Mos whare, arta, dres an mor
Dh'aga threvow may-tethons
Po dhe'n keynvorow, aga nor.

They were perching, some of them, above on masts, straight and upright; but these were only perches for a moment, for boats do not stay long in harbours.

The little boats soon had to go back across the sea to their homes from whence they came, or to the oceans, their familiar world.

J.A.N. Snell (Gwas Kevardhu) 1938–

Mys Du

An newl tawesek tewl a goth
   ow pludhia cuth an vledhen glaf
in cudh; en lyth gwedhennow noth.

   Ha brottel yu'n ughelder braf
terris diworth an dher'wen ven:
   an gwinsow tin yu gwarnias gwaf.

Scorennow lom ha crom in cren
   a scravin skethennow comol los
i'n enef y wheth an awel yen.

   Y crighyll pren podrethek i'n cos,
prisclow ha plisk yu gwisk an lur
   ha faclow a danflam adrif an fos.

Glawennow glew yu dagrow dur
   ow quana croghen gwilliow wan:
mes ogas dh'y olas an pollat fur.

   Linak an lanergh a lorgan splan
ow fenna, lyf yenhes, disliw:
   y cren an vran billennek in ban.

Linnow ha resiow lisak a rew,
   cales ha perillis an trulergh:
res yu omgeles a'n orwins glew.

An Helgh

War an vron, war an meneth,
my re bonias oll an jeth
   ha rip an mor
— ow whegoll, kemer trueth! –
mes dha gafos war an dreth
   ow wherthin clor.

Myrgh ow sewia scovarnek
byth ny welis-vy mar whek
   ha mar heblith;

J.A.N. Snell (Gwas Kevardhu) 1938–

November

The dark quiet mist falls, soothing the grief of the sick year in a soft veil of naked trees.

And fragile is the fine mistletoe broken off by the stout oak: the bitter winds are a warning of winter.

Bare and bent quivering branches scratch rags of grey cloud: in my soul blows the cold wind.

A rotten tree quakes in the wood, pods and bark are the clothing of the ground and kindling flame behind the wall.

Translucent drops of rain are steel tears, stabbing the skin of weak beggars: but the sensible fellow will be near to his hearth.

Patterned is the glade with bright moonlight overflowing, a flood cold and pale: the ragged crow quivers aloft.

Lakes and muddy streams freeze, hard and dangerous is the path: it is necessary to hide from the keen cold wind.

Lakes and muddy streams freeze, hard and dangerous is the path: it is necessary to hide from the keen cold wind.

The Hunt

On the hill, on the mountain, I have run throughout the day, and by the sea – my sweetheart, have pity! – just to find you on the beach and laugh gently.

I never saw a girl so beautiful following a hare, or so supple; stopping, tired, in a

ow hedhi squith in gwelsek
rag golghi 'dan fenten dek
   hy diwvogh ruth.

Neb eos tont i'n spedhes,
hy a wruk anedhi ges
   ha hy 'dan gel:
dhe wyr y lammas piskes
splan aga fennow i'n skes
   rip glan an gwel.

A bup trulergh ha nonnen
may whruga fiski yn fen
   ny borthaf cof:
esedhin war an drethen –
amma dhim na wra nahen;
   dianal of.

Pyu a Vyn Prena Breten?

Lemmyn, a dus jentyl dha,
geseugh dhym dh'ombresentya:
lewyth un gowethas vur
gans scor yn lyes randyr.
Predereugh, mar plek, un dra
us a vern dheugh y'n urma...
pandr'us lemmyn y'gas brys
yn kever agas erbys?
Agas arghans-why a wra
po tevy po dyfygya;
nyns us scusy vytholl dheugh.
Na wreugh trynya: ervyreugh!
Dhymmo vy cryseugh, hep wow,
stokkys ha randalosow,
dafar ha taclow hen druth,
lywansow, – ny dal travyth.
Cleweugh lemmyn, my a wra
leverel dheugh towl gwella.
Why a yl bos, dredhon ny,
perghen nebes erewy:
ran vyan a Vreten Vur
a vyth dhewhy hep preder.
Y dalvesygeth a vyth
par hap encressyes canquyth
erbyn agas mernans why!
Y'n urma ny res tylly,

patch of grass to wash in a
lovely spring, her red
cheeks.

Some impertinent nightin-
gale in a thicket made mock
of her from its hiding place:
in truth, fish leaped, their
heads bright in the shadow
by the bank of the field.

I do not recall every footpath
and stream where I rushed:
let us sit down on the sand –
kiss me, and nothing else: I
am breathless.

Who Will Buy Britain?

Now, good gentlemen, permit
me to introduce myself, presi-
dent of a large company with
branches in many regions.
Think, if you please, about
one thing which concerns you
now: what have you in mind
with regard to your savings?
Your money will either grow
or decline; for you there is no
avoiding it. Do not delay:
decide! Believe me, without a
lie, stocks and shares, pre-
cious antiques, paintings –
they are worth nothing. Here,
now, I will tell you of a better
scheme. You can be, through
us, owner of a few acres: a lit-
tle part of Great Britain will
be yours without anxiety.
Perhaps its value will have
increased a hundred times by
your death! It is not necessary
to pay now, but study this
booklet: and behold, you are

mes, studhyeugh an lyfryk ma:
hag ot, why yu an kensa
y'n resekva bryntyn bras
dhe gafos agas gweras.
(Ha why yu pell adherak
an oylbennow Arabyak!)
Avel plans yn mes a'n pry
y whra 'gas arghans tevy;
avel delyow kynyaf hel
punsow a wra omguntell!
Ha mar mynnough, byth ny res
dhewhy dhe vos gweles
agas pastel dyr, mar bell
kyn fo: y fyth dyogel,
po gwresen, po gonyow gwak,
po menedhek, po cosak.
'Glewseugh a Securicor?
Henna nyns yu kesstryfor
herwyth agan meny-ny
nep re wruk ty dhe synsy
agas rychys-why yn tyn
gans lu ervys ha brathcun.
Kyn fo corwyns, teweth fell,
kyn fo terros has gustel,
ny a wra 'gas gwytha sur
rak drok an Bagas Lafur!

An Lef Mes a'n Mor

(Selyes war henwhethel kernewek)

Pyscajor yth esa
    yn tewlder ow mos
war drethow Por' Towan
    wor' golow an nos.

Y clewas un spyrys
    ow crya yn yen:
'An ur yu devedhys,
    na nyns yu an den.'

An lor a wolowys
    an carrygy hen.
'An ur yu devedhys,
    na nyns yu an den.'

the first in the great wonderful race to win your soil. (And you are far in front of the Arabian olearchs!) Like a plant your money will grow out of the earth; like the leaves of a generous harvest pounds will gather! And if you so desire, it will never be necessary for you to go and see your land, however remote it may be it will be safe, be it fertile ground or empty downs, mountainous, or wooded. Have you heard of Securicor? They are no competition compared to our company, which has sworn to hold your wealth firmly with an armed host and mastiffs. Though there be whirlwind, bad weather, though there be disaster and riot, we will keep you secure from the wickedness of the Labour Party!

The Voice out of the Sea

(Based on an ancient Cornish legend)

There was a fisherman,
going in the darkness onto
the beaches of Porthtowan,
in the light of the moon.

He heard a spirit crying out
coldly: 'The hour has come,
and the man has not.'

The moon lit the ancient
rocks: 'The hour has come,
and the man has not.'

Ha tergwyth y'n awel
   an lef a dhassen:
'An ur yu devedhys,
    na nyns yu an den.'

Ynter an comol
   ha gwartha an vron
tarosvan yn cugol
   a sevy hep son.

An gwyns a greghyllys
   y won truan du;
y fyas war woles
   yn newlen dhyslyw.

Hag ena nyns esa
   saw golow an lor,
ha dewyn ow crenna
   war donnow an mor.

Chy War an Als

Degeugh an darras yn clos
erbyn an gowas los
adrus an mor ow tos,
kepar ha ky conneryek
adro dhe'n chy ow resek.

Gwreugh nessa dhe'gas olas,
kemereugh powes a'gas palas,
geseugh dhe gusca'n gweras:
lemmyn tanneugh an prys
hedra vo gwyn agas bys.

Why re sowynnas yn sur
wosa caletter mur
ha boghosekter pur,
ow tysquedhes agas gwrydhyow
yn tyreth ughel ha garow.

Yn le lynas, why re vegys
breghesow blejyow melys:
melyon, lyly-Corawys,
salow aga gwryth y'n dor
'dan bern agas dywla clor.
Why re dhyndylas yn whyr

And three times in the wind,
the voice echoes: 'The hour
has come, and the man has
not.'

Between the clouds and the
top of the hill stood an
apparition in a hood, without
a sound.

The wind shook its pitiful
black gown; it fled down-
wards into a pale bank of
mist.

And then there was only the
light of the moon, its ray
quivering on the waves of the
sea.

House on the Cliff

Shut the door tight against the
grey shower which is coming
across the sea, running like a
rabid dog about the house.

Draw near to your hearth, take
a rest from your digging, let
the soil sleep: take the time
now while you are happy.

You have succeeded well after
great hardship and real pover-
ty, showing your roots in a
high and harsh territory.

In the place of nettles, you
have raised armfuls of sweet
flowers: violets, Lent lilies,
with roots safe in the earth
under the care of your gentle
hands.

haneth un hunas hur
yn cosoleth agas tyr.
Mes haneth ny wra'n awel
na powes un cors na tewel.

An noswyth oll 'ma'n gwynsow
ow trehevel tarosvannow
aberth y'gas hunrosow –
cowethyas yn gwary-myr
asper, galarus ha hyr.

Gorrans an gwary ma yu plen
gwastas yn cyta yen:
ottawhy a'gas saf yn cres
yn dan dour ughel unyk
serth, tanow, gwynnyk.

Y'n whetegves lur awotta
benen goth ow carma –
re bell, re bell awartha,
scant ny glewyr hy lef
a ugh an awel cref.

Hy thremyn truesy gwyn
adryf fenester yn
a re dheugh ponow tyn:
an enep ma lyesegwyth
why re'n gwelas, why a'n gwelvyth.

Why a dheth omma dh'ankevy
cavow, ancombrynsy,
ha tervans an cyta truesy.
Dhe hunros noweth splan
why a wruk omwul yn lan.

Prag y tyfunough yn trom,
maga pos avel plom,
owth ola dagrow tom?
Byth na sconyeugh an hunlef:
cryow cuth agas enef.

Kyn fo deges an darras,
y te pup nos owth hanas,
der an crygow ow cramyas,
awel tanow yn scus:
levow tryst agas tus.

You have indeed earned a long sleep tonight in the quietness of your land. But tonight the wind does not rest a moment or quieten.

Throughout the night the winds raise spectres within your dreams – a companion in a harsh, painful and long drama.

The setting of this drama is a level amphitheatre in a cold city; here you are standing in the middle, under a high lowly straight tower, thin and pale.

Behold on the sixteenth floor an old woman crying out – too far, too far up, her voice is scarcely heard above the strong wind.

Her pitiful weak face behind a narrow window gives you deep pain: many times you have seen and will see this face.

You came here to forget the anxieties and perplexity and racket of the doleful city. You dedicated yourself entirely to a brand new dream.

Why do you awaken so suddenly, as heavy as lead, weeping hot tears? Never deny the nightmare, the secret cries of your soul.

Although the door is shut, it comes sighing every night, creeping through the cracks, a keen wind in shadow: the sad voices of your people.

Jonathan

*(Jonathan Page a ve budhys yn 1972,
yn canoe ogas dhe Geresk, ha ganso 19
bloth)*

Glaw hager yma haneth
yn dagrow yeyn hep deweth.
Gallas pell un coweth freth.

Glaw hager ha golow gwan:
ny wodhyen myras yn ban
pan ve budhys Jonathan.

Glaw hager, naswedhow glew
ow quana ewon ton du
a dheghesas y gorf brew.

Howl gosruth godom ha whar
ow tywy dha enep huth:
covath dha vedhelhe cuth.

Howl gosruth war garrek vur
may whrussta 'skynna yn fur:
golok mar dhruth whath y'm cur.

Avon uskys pell a'n mor,
scath byan, ha revador –
ken cof ylyn my a bor'.

Avon uskys, tonnow bew,
scathow cul ha scaf yn rew;
ha dha gana my a glew.

Avon uskys a'th tynyas,
ty gar gwyn ha'th cowethas
yn rak dhe'n keynvor ahas.

Golow gwyn, pras efan ergh:
oll ny eth y'n gonyow gwergh
ow whylas ol an trulergh.

Glow gwyn y'n col ughel
a wanas dha dheulagas fel;
ow whythra lyn an gorwel.

Jonathan

(Jonathan Page was drowned in 1972, in a canoe near Exeter, at the age of 19.)

There is harsh rain tonight in tears without end. A lively friend has gone far.

There is harsh rain and weak light: I could not look up when Jonathan was drowned.

Harsh rain, translucent needles stabbing the foam of a black wave which struck his bruised body.

Blood-red warm and gentle sun illuminating your merry face: a memory to soften grief.

Blood-red sun on a great rock where you climbed skilfully: a sight precious in my care.

A fast river far from the sea, a small boat, and a rower – another dear memory I recall.

A fast river, lively waves, narrow and light boats in a row; and your singing I hear.

A fast river attracted you, fair friend, and your companions, onwards to the hateful ocean.

Bright light, a broad meadow of snow: we all went to the virginal downs to seek traces of the path.

Bright light in the zenith stabbed your cunning eyes; scanning the line of the horizon.

Golow gwyn y'n crybow splan
a den ow lagas yn ban.
Dew genes, a Jonathan

An Ros

Y re dhyscudhas ros-dowr aral hen
Maglys yn pry ha dreys ha gossen.
Ha'm ewyn vy ow cravas an gammek,
bys y'n dyns y clewaf galar skethrek.

Hunros jynnor muskegys dhym yma
ha pump ow tyfygya 'dan y dhywla,
ha'y gowetha ow taga ottensy
pell war woles y'n pol ow pudhy.

Eskern yma, encledhyes y'gan tyr
ow cortos dasserghy ha gwysca styr:
ye, re anedha 'ma yn golow deth
mes whath y's teves sawor claf an beth.

Arwedhow lowr yma, mes scullyes yns:
banerow dybowes fregys y'n gwyns.
Res gwya warbarth an nujow yn ten,
mun-lywyws: du ha gwyn ha ruthvelen.

Levow lowr yma, byrth war an alsyow
ow carma serrys erbyn an tonnow,
gwylanas gwyls yn kesstryf tyn a van:
res yu dhedha omguntell yn kescan.

Na berthyn own a dhalghenna'n estren
ha mortholya y dhywscovarn yn fen
dre whethlow agan tyr hep dyharas.
Y gyfy gwren: y whrava godhvos gras.

Hun-desempys yu agan cleves cas.
An cuscajor re blynchyas y lagas,
dyanowy, hedhes luf ha lefa,
ha res yu dhyn omlath dh'y dhyfuna.

Prederyn, drefen nag us termyn lowr.
Res yu dhyn gul trelya dhe'n rosow-dowr:
y halsa hy bos martesen un forth
dhe herdhya gos dre wythy pobel worth.

Bright light in the shining crests draw
my eyes upwards. God with you,
Jonathan.

The Wheel

They have discovered another old water wheel,
tangled in clay and briars and rust. As my nail
scratches the rim, I feel a splintered pain right
into my teeth.

I have a dream of a mad engineer, and a pump
failing under his hands, and behold his friends,
stifling, drowning far below in the pit.

Bones there are, buried in our land, waiting to
rise again and put on meaning: there are some
in the light of day, but still they have the sick
odour of the grave.

Signs enough there are, but they are scattered:
restless flags frayed in the wind. It is necessary
to weave the threads tightly together, ore-
coloured: black and white and saffron.

Voices enough there are, poets on the cliffs
shouting angrily against the waves, wild sea-
gulls in a fierce struggle above: they must gath-
er in a chorus.

Let us not fear to grab hold of the stranger and
strenuously hammer his ears with legends of
our land, without apologising. Let us forgive
him: he will thank us.

Lethargy is our hateful sickness. The sleeper
has blinked his eye, yawned, stretched out a
hand and cried aloud, and we must fight to
awaken him.

Let us think, for there is not enough time. We
must make the water-wheels turn: it could per-
haps be a way to drive blood through the veins
of a stubborn people.

N.J.A. Williams (Golvan) 1942–

[Lowsys yu Logh Lagas Glas]

Lowsys yu logh lagas glas
ganow gwyn gensy gallas
ny bew bennath ha mollath meth
a calses clewes dhys canen
ha devra dagrow dughan.

[Marthus Bras yu Margh Bryntyn]

Marthus bras yu margh bryntyn
prest ow squytha pup skennyn
mes aneth moy es nerth men
mowes lel na moren len.

[Gwaynten 'ma yn Breten Vyghan]

Gwaynten 'ma yn Breten Vyghan
Trelys yu an vledhen ros
    Eythyn tek banal melen
A gweth pup tu an ros
Gans tonnow splan lemmyn y can
    An gucu der an cos.

Gwak yu an hens, gweles den-vyth
    Ny yller yn nep le
Mes an byasen lowenek
    A nyj adro dhe'n ke
Hy fluf du ha glas ha gwyn
    A lever bos haf de.

N.J.A. Williams (Golvan) 1942–

[Dulled is the Lake of a Blue Eye]

Dulled is the lake of a blue eye, fair
mouth gone for lost; blessing and curs-
ing have no shame: if you could hear, I
should sing to you and shed tears of
melancholy.

[Wondrous Great is a Noble Stallion]

Wondrous great is a noble stallion, constant-
ly straining every sinew; but a greater wonder
than brute strength is a faithful girl or a trust-
worthy maid.

[It is Spring in Brittany]

It is Spring in Brittany, the wheel of
the year has turned, and fair furze
and yellow bloom dress every part
of the heath: with glorious tunes
now sings the cuckoo through the
wood.

Empty is the road, not a single per-
son can be seen anywhere; but the
merry magpie flies round the
hedge, her black and blue and
white plumage say that summer
will come.

[Bryntyn o Breten Ow Thas]

Bryntyn o Breten ow thas
bro gwelyow ha brynyow glas
rak blam lemmyn war wels bluth
'trehevyr ruth trevow uth.

Kynyaf

An frut re bu cuntellys,
ow codha 'ma an del;
an newl a wra omlesa;
ot! ass yu ber an gwel.

An gwaf a dhe hep lettya,
an ayr yu nebes yeyn.
Fysk ha gwra degea
an darras war dha geyn

Devedhys yu mys Hedra,
y fyth mys Du yn scon;
mar qura nefra dyfuna
ow gwlas-vy my ny won.

Dhe Gof Mordon

Glan y golon, glan y gel;
mynnas mon ganso medhel;
pensergh dhodho hengof dek
kescows cosel Kernow;
bardhonyeth an yeth
a barusys: y bregeth
o sevel tan cyvylta
Kernow Goth, coron gwyth
agan len o gyllys hyr
may fe cof mayth ankevyr.
Ancof dhyn byner re bo:
nef pysyn cof may pesyo.

[Noble was the Britain of My Father]

Noble was the Britain of my father, a land
of green hills and fields; but, for shame,
now on the tender grass are built a crowd of
fearsome towns.

Autumn

The fruit has been gath-
ered, the leaves are falling,
the mist spreads around;
behold! how short is sight.

The winter will come with-
out delay, the air is some-
what cold. Hurry and shut
the door behind you.

October is come, it will
soon be November; I do not
know if my country will
ever wake.

In Memory of Mordon[1]

Pure his heart, pure his secret, he
had a keen and tender desire; his
greatest love was for the lovely tradi-
tion of the quiet speech of Cornwall;
poetry he prepared; his sermon was
to raise the fire of Old Cornwall's
culture to keep the crown of your lit-
erature which was long gone, so
that there will be remembrance
instead of forgetting. May he never
be forgotten; let us pray Heaven that
the memory of him lasts.

Scusow[2]

Yn cres an cos y whelys
scusow, hag yth aswonys
aga bos an dus wyrra;
an gwyth gans del y a gweth
yu melen ha gwer y'n jeth
an gwaynten pan vo omma.

Gans an bys re omledhys
ha gruthyl travyth ny yllys;
my a drelyas ow threys-vy
dhe golselder tek an cos
gans y dus scusow y'n nos
ow quandra aragof-vy.
Tarosvan ough-why ow thull
hep defnyth na corf a scull
yn dan wolow an lor len
scus war dhor glyp ha'n gwels bluth
yu megys yn fyn gans ruth
an scusow aga honen.

A ylta hunrosa, scus
maga ta avel an dus
a'n bys claf-ma hep spyrys
bardhonyeth y'ga enef?
A ylta gans ster an nef
kewsel a'n pyth a vern dhys?

Scus! deryf dhym kerensa
Dew agan tas awartha.
Gormeleugh-ef hep anken
may hyllyf-vy dascafos
ow cryjyans dhodho y'n cos
kellys del welyn mapden.

Nyns yu Ma's Ges a Wraf [esrann]

Milites
Ogh, ogh, ny re be fethys!
Tremena Tamar uskys
    'Vya gwell dhyn.
An Gernewyon bos pur wan
a dalvya. Nyns ens man

Shadows

In the middle of the wood I saw shadows, and I knew that they were the truest people; they clothe the trees in leaves which are yellow and green in the day when the spring is here.

I have fought with the world, and not been able to do anything; I turned my feet to the beautiful quiet of the wood with its people, the shadows in the night, wandering in front of me. A phantom you are, my disappointment, without substance or a body which throws under the light of the faithful moon a shadow on wet earth and the soft grass which is cared for delicately by a crowd of the shades themselves.

Can you dream, shadow, as well as the people in this sick world without the spirit of poetry in their souls? Can you speak with the stars of heaven about that which concerns you?

Shadow! Proclaim to me the love of God our Father above. Praise him without fear, so that I can find again my faith in him in the wood, as I see mankind lost.

I'm Only Making Fun [extract]

Soldiers.
Woe, woe, we have been defeated! It would be better for us to cross the Tamar quickly. The Cornishmen were meant to be very weak. They

mes cref ha tyn.

Owt! Harow! Harow! Harow!
Kyn ven ledhys ha marow
ny a vyn mos dres Tamar.
Nyns us forth aral y'n bys,
mar trygyn bydhyn ledhys
gans an Gernewyon hep mar.

fugiunt milites tunc pompabit sacerdos et dicet

Sacerdos
My yu devedhys hep wow
mayth encledhyer tus varow
ha ragtha gonys eglos.
Owth omlath sul ve ledhys
abarth Kernow murgerys
dens yn rak dhym hep gortos.

Bardus Magnus
Mar plek, ow ascusya gwra
mes goky os, pronter da.
Ny yl tus varow dyson
dones yn rak genes may fons
encledhyes gans lun revrons.
Ledhys re bons gans Sawson.

Sacerdos
Gwyr yu an ger a gewsyth,
skyansek os, a lewyth,
mes y res kyn fe hy nos
oll an dus ma ancledhya
poken bydhons ow flerya
y'gan deufryk sawor pos.

Gwreugh ytho beth ragtha-y
omma y'n dor dhymmo-vy
    ha dre wonys
an Eglos sans my a wra
oll an corvow encledhya
    yn pur uskys.

Bardus Magnus
A'gas bus why gwyr y'n bys
a wul hemma? Yma res
    dhys leverel
pandra yu agas hanow
ha pyth ough hep falladow,

were not at all, but strong and
fierce.

Alas, help, help, help! Though
we should be killed and dead
we will cross the Tamar. There
is no other way in the world, if
we stay we shall be killed by
the Cornish without doubt.

The soldiers flee and a priest appears, saying

Priest
I have come, without a lie, so
that the dead may be buried
and a service celebrated for
them. Whoever was slain
fighting for greatly-loved
Cornwall, let him come for-
ward to me without delay.

Grand Bard
Excuse me, please, but you
are foolish, good priest. Dead
people certainly cannot come
forward so that they may be
buried by you with full
respect. They have been slain
by Saxons.

Priest
True is the word you speak,
you are wise, O leader, but it is
necessary before night to bury
all these people, or else they
will be stinking with a heavy
odour in our nostrils.

Make for them a grave in the
earth and through the service
of the holy Church I will bury
all these bodies very quickly.

Grand Bard
Have you any right in the
world to do that? You must tell
me what is your name and

Dew dhe'th sylwel!

Sacerdos
Jowan Tregeare of whare.
A Newlyn Est my a dhe
  rag encledhyans.
Ny yu pronter an Eglos.
Mar ny'n gwelyth, goky os,
  pur wyr dhyblans.

Bardus Magnus
Agas bos pronter gwyryon
my a wel lemmyn dyson.
  Encledhya gwra
oll an corvow-ma ytho
sawor wherow ma na vo
  vyth oll omma.

fodient fossam et ponent corpora in fossam

Sacerdos
Frontis tuo sudore
tu vesces tuo pane
donec in terram rursus
pulverem revertis
de quo olim es sumptus.

A Dhew tas ollgallosek
a'gan Arluth Jesu whek
gwra benyga an beth-ma
may fo dhe'th servysy lel
omma powesva gosel
ha growethva whek dhedha.

Dre dha vap an keth Jhesu
bewnans benygys del yu
ha dasserghyans dh'y dus len
nep a rewl gans syns nefra
ha'n Spyrys Sans magata
un Drynsys trank hep worfen.

what you are without fail, God save you!

Priest
John Tregeare[3] am I indeed, from Newlyn East I come for a burial. I am a priest of the Church. If you see it not, you are foolish, that is obvious.

Grand Bard
That you are a true priest I see now clearly. Do you bury all these bodies then, so that there will not be any bitter smell here.

They dig a ditch and put the bodies in the ditch

Priest
You shall gain your bread by the sweat of your brow until you return to the earth, for from it you were taken. O God the Father Almighty of our Lord sweet Jesus, bless this grave, so that there may be to these your faithful servants a quiet resting place and sweet repose for them.

As there is through your son the same Jesus blessed life and resurrection for his faithful people, who rules with the saints forever and the Holy Ghost as well, one Trinity age without end.

Maylura [esrann]

Maylura
Howel hag Alwar marow!
Trystys bras dhe dus Kernow
   ha dhymmo-vy.
Fatel vewaf-vy heptha?
Gallas ow bewnans gansa
   yn pur dhefry.

My a'th cara Howel tek
hebos oma anfusek
   ha ty ledhys.
Ha ty Alwar lel esta
dhymmo surly y'n ur-ma
   pan vuf sconys.

Galsough agas deu dhe ves
a Vaylura myghternes
   dysenorys.
Howel unkynda ty o,
Alwar, hegar es dhymmo,
   ynweth kerys.

An yl gans y gyla ve
ledhys, gans y vroder e',
   ogh! namna der
ynnof ow holon; nefra
ny wraf ma's ola ragtha
   del ens dhym ker.

Oleugh, halow tyr Kernow
aga deu bones marow!
   Deu lyon ens ...

Maylura [extract]

Maylura

Howel and Alwar[4] dead! A great sadness to the people of Cornwall and to me. How shall I live without them? Life is gone with them truly.

I loved you, fair Howel. Without you I am unfortunate, and you slain. And you, Alwar, were faithful to me indeed in the hour when I was rejected.

You have both gone from Maylura, dishonoured queen. Howel, you were ungrateful; Alwar, you were loving towards me, and I loved you.

The one was killed by the other, by his own brother, woe! My heart almost breaks within me; I shall never do anything but weep for them, so dear were they to me.

Weep, moors of the land of Cornwall, for they are both dead! Two lions they were ...

Julyan Holmes (Blew Melen) 1948–

Kerth Kernowyon

An tyr nyns yu ankevys
Kynth us cows y vos marow,
Mes scon y fyth drehevys
Rak sevel dybarow;
Yowynk ha los, gwren ny oll dos
   War-barth a golon gref:
Treveglos ha porth, kemeryn an forth,
   Ha kenyn a ughel lef –
      Pypynag oll a grys dhe goll
        Bos gyllys Kernow ger,
      Gwrens y gothvos y whren mos
        War rak, gans spyrys ter!

Na bythqueth ny ankevyn,
Po ny a gren a'gan barvow,
Agan lel wellhevyn
A borth browt arvow:
Gerens ha Margh, Costentyn, Dongarth
   A synsy fay'n dan Nef,
Ha bys vynytha, ny a vyn y wytha,
   Ha'y gana yn ughel lef:
      Pypynag oll a grys dhe goll
        Bos gyllys Kernow ger,
      Gwrens y gothvos y whren mos
        War rak, gans spyrys ter!

Nyns yu an dus ankevys
Kens a wytha war an tyr:
Y fyth aga spyrys
Gans pup den lel ha gwyr:
Gwren perthy cof a Vyghal an Gof,
   A Flamank ha Trelawny cref:
Gans aga nerth, yn rak ny a gerth,
   Ha dhe'n Saws gul clewes 'gan lef.
      Pypynag oll a grys dhe goll
        Bos gyllys Kernow ger,
      Gwrens y gothvos y whren mos
        War rak, gans spyrys ter!

Julyan Holmes (Blew Melen) 1948–

Cornishmen's March

The land is not forgotten although there is talk of its being dead, but soon it will be raised to stand peerless; young and old, let us all come together with strong hearts: church town and port, let us take the road, and let us sing with a loud voice:
Whoever believes that dear Cornwall is lost, let him know we will go forward, with eager spirit!

Nor let us ever forget, or we shall shake in our beards, our faithful princes who bear glorious arms: Gerontius and Mark, Constantine, Donierts who kept faith under heaven, and for ever more, we shall keep it, and sing with a loud voice:
Whoever believes that dear Cornwall is lost, let him know we will go forward, with eager spirit!

The men who once guarded the land are not forgotten; their spirit will be with every faithful man: let us remember Michael the Smith, Flamank, and strong Trelawny: with their strength, forward we march, and make the Saxon hear our voice:
Whoever believes that dear Cornwall is lost, let him know we will go forward, with eager spirit!

Tim Saunders (Bardh Gwerin) 1952–

Hunrosen

Dylyow an vlejen yn dan an ergh
A wôr pan vyth prys lemmel,
Prys eskynna ha prys nyja,
Ur dhe dardha
Hag ur dhe rowedha a-hes.

Y re glewas jag pup erghen
A-ban vu budhys Mys Kevardhu,
Galsons cales aga holonow
Erbyn profusans
Golowyn a sythlas an ayr.

Ny wodhons, ha ny's dur man
A vyth badus an has
Yn dan garnow horn
An Gwaynten,
Ha hungana y a wruk agensow.

Kasa Ha Kara

Teir thra dreus oll a'gasav:
Pell wortos traen yn gworsav;
Esow dowr der oll an hav;
Te yein dre weilenn galav.

Tri gwin ny's tÿvonz haval:
Cneuz fyrv hag adhvez aval;
Bleuzyow cann scaw tiredh sal;
Ha gwaneth melynn manal.

Drolla

Y'n termyn usy tremenys
Y têth tri marnor yowynk
Adhi-worth an cay
Bys y'n dewottŷ ma.
Pup huni yn ŷ dro,

Tim Saunders (Bardh Gwerin) 1952–

Dream Rose

The petals of the flower beneath
the snow know when it is time to
leap, time to rise and time to fly,
the hour to burst and the hour to
lie down.

They have felt the jolt of every
snowflake since December was
drowned, they have become hard-
hearted against the prophecy of a
ray of light filtered by the air.

They do not know, and they do not
care that the seed will be stupefied
under the iron hooves of the
Spring, and they have just sung a
lullaby.

Loving and Hating

There are three things that I hate particular-
ly: waiting for a long time at the station for a
train; a shortage of water throughout the
summer; cold tea through a straw.

Three kinds of wine are without equal: the
firm and mature flesh of an apple; the snow-
white flowers of elder trees from salty land;
and yellow wheat in a stook.

Tale

In the time that is past,
there came three
young seamen from
the quayside into this
pub. Each one in his

Perna a wrens tennow
A goref an ŷl dh' ŷ gila.
Y canens nebes canow,
Leverel nebes whethligow lik,
Ha worteweth
Sevel rak vodya.
Drê wall
Yth herdhyas onen anedha
Un loncor a' ŷ hens,
Hag omgnoukya a wruk an dhow
A-berth yn kelgh a armow
Erna dhêth an gefnisoryon
Dhe derri dresta
Ha terri aga fennow
Er-byn tenewan carven glâs.
Onen whath
A'n tri marnor
A gôdhas wosa pymp mis
Bys yn hyli stronk
Porth tramor
Yntra gorghel ha cay,
Ha'n tressa a dremenas
Deth ha hanter
Ow scriva lyther
Dh' ŷ wrêk.
Wosa deweth an trumach
Yth êth dh' ŷ gweles
Yn hŷ chŷ-cusul
A-wartha Por' la.
Hŷ mam re dhothya
Dhe wul gweres
Miras an baban,
Hag y leveri hŷ whoer
Na dalv ŷa
'Fors fatel vo
Priosa marnor.
Y follothas an coweth
Perghnogyon gorholyon
Hag y coscas an wedhowes yowynk
Hŷ whoer.
Dhodho êf
Y kemeras
Hyhí cumyas tek
War an truthow
Yn mysk sawthan
An gentrevogyon.
Hag otomma
Deweth ow drolla.

turn bought beer for the others. They sang a few songs, told a few dirty jokes, and at last got up to leave. Accidentally one of them pushed a certain regular out of his way, and the two boxed away within a circle of shouts until the police came to interrupt them and break their heads against the side of a blue van. Another one of the three seamen fell five months later into the polluted brine of a foreign harbour, and the third spent a day and a half writing a letter to his wife. After the end of the voyage he went to see her in her council house above St. Ives. Her mother had come to help look after the baby, and her sister said that it wasn't worth marrying a seaman anyway. The friend cursed shipowners and the young widow gave her sister a telling-off. It was he to whom she bid a warm farewell on the doorstep amidst the neighbours' astonishment. And here is the end of my tale.

Biographies

John Davey 1812–91

Farmer and mathematician from Zennor. He was the son of a celebrated teacher of the same name.

Crankan/Cranken. Collected by John Hobson Matthews, historian of St Ives district, in 1891. Davey told him that it had come down in his family.

Georg Sauerwein 1831–1903

Sauerwein was born in Gronau in northern Germany. A gifted linguist, he spent much of his life working as a Biblical translator. He also campaigned for the rights of minorities, including those under German rule. He wrote poetry in several languages, and a collection of his poems in Sorbian, a Slavic language spoken in eastern Germany, was published in the 1970s. He came into contact with Celtic languages while working in the household in Gwent of Lady Llanover, an active patron of Welsh language and culture.

Edwin Norris/Edwin Norris; Cowyth Ker, dhe dhen Claf/Dear Friend, to a Sick Man. These poems were published in *Kernow,* 1933.

Henry Jenner (Gwas Myghal – Servant of Michael) 1848–1934

During his courtship of Katharine Rawlings (better known as the poet and novelist Kitty Lee) of Hayle in the 1870s Jenner became aware of the oral traditions of Cornish in Penwith and in the course of a long career at the British Museum Library he discovered a fragment from the only known secular text in Middle Cornish. By bringing the oral and manuscript traditions together, he would eventually initiate the Cornish Revival with his *Handbook of the Cornish Language* (1904). This book, based on the dialects of Penwith and Kerrier, but with the spelling regularised in accordance with the phonetic transcriptions of the great Welsh scholar Edward Lluyd (1660–1709), would be the basis of standard Cornish for some twenty years. It includes a chapter on versification, in which Jenner briefly describes the poetic techniques of the traditional literature, and advocates a combination of these and general European prosody. He sought affirmation of Cornwall's identity in the wider Celtic world and worked for many years to have a Cornish Gorseth, or Order of Bards, established as in Wales and Brittany. Towards the end of his life he became a Roman Catholic.

Bro Goth Agan Tasow/Ancient Land of Our Fathers. Leaflet printed by the author, 1904.
Devedhyans an Matern/The Coming of the King. Published in *Celtia,* 1904.
Dhô'm Gwreg Gernûak/To My Cornish wife. Published in the *Handbook of the Cornish Language,* 1904.
An Pemthak Pell/ The Fifteen Bezants. Manuscript c.1904. Jenner papers, Courtney Library , Royal Institution of Cornwall, Truro.
Can Wlascar Agan Mamvro/Patriotic Song of the Motherland. Manuscript, c.1904. Jenner papers, Courtney Library, Royal Institution of Cornwall, Truro.

L. R. C. Duncombe-Jewell (Barth Glas – Blue Bard) 1866–19?

Duncombe-Jewell was the moving spirit behind the short-lived but influential Celto-Cornish

Society at the turn of the century. It was he who persuaded Jenner to make his knowledge of Cornish available to the general public in the form of the *Handbook* and led the vigorous campaign that persuaded the Celtic Congress to recognise Cornwall.

Mychternes, Mychternes an Eleth Dhus! Queen, Queen of the Angels, Come! Published in *Celtia*, 1901.

C. A. Picquenard (Ar Barz Melen – The Fair-Haired Bard) 1872–1940

Picquenard's influence on Jenner's ideas was crucial in setting the course of the Cornish movement. A doctor by profession, Picquenard was active in the growing Breton movement, which saw Breton identity as based on an integration of faith, language and race. Jenner wanted to transfer this paradigm to Cornwall. In the chapter on versification in his *Handbook of the Cornish Language* Jenner mentions Picquenard as someone who has already started to write poetry in Cornish.

An Nef Kellys/The Lost Heaven. Published in *Celtia*, 1902.

Robert Morton Nance (Mordon – Sea Wave) 1873–1959

Morton Nance trained as an artist under Sir Hubert von Herkomer, who designed the regalia of the Welsh Gorsedd. His parents belonged to the flourishing Cornish community in Cardiff and gave him a consuming fascination with all aspects of Cornish culture. After his marriage, Nance settled in Cornwall and devoted the rest of his life to working for its language and culture. His collaboration with Jenner began towards the end of the First World War. To Jenner's antiquarian image of Cornwall he added a vision based upon popular culture and the historical experience of the Industrial Revolution. As well as realising Jenner's project of founding a Cornish Gorseth, he also founded the Federation of Old Cornwall Societies, dedicated to the preservation of Cornish culture. His dictionaries and grammar, based on the spelling and usage of Middle Cornish, but incorporating much material from the Early Modern period, are still used by many people.

Nyns yu Marow Maghtern Arthur/King Arthur Is Not Dead! Published in *Old Cornwall,* 1927.
Arta Ef A-Dhe/He Shall Come Again. Published in the Gorseth ritual, 1929.
Dynergh Dhe Dus A Vreten Vyghan and *Yeghes Da Dhe'n Myghtern!/ Good Health to the King!*. Published in the *Cornish Songbook*, 1929.
An Margh Coth/The Old Horse. Published in *Old Cornwall*, 1932.
An Edhen Huder/The Magical Bird. Manuscript c. 1932. Papers of Robert Morton Nance, Courtney Library, Royal Institution of Cornwall, Truro.
An Dullores/The Deceitful Girl. Published in *Old Cornwall*, 1940.
An Vowes Doth/The Wise Girl. Published in *Old Cornwall*, 1934.

R. St. V. Allin-Collins (Hal Wyn – White Moor) 1878–19?

Commercial translator, working in the City of London. Widely read in the literatures of the Celtic and many other languages, he spoke Cornish fluently and held informal Cornish sessions at his office in Fenchurch Street. During the 1930s he incurred the displeasure of Morton Nance and other figures of the Revival, who took to informing editors that his usage of Cornish was unauthorised. Much of his correspondence is preserved in the Courtney Library, at the Royal Institution of Cornwall, Truro..

Hal Wyn/ Hal Wyn. Manuscript c.1935. Private collection.
Moren a'n Pow/A Maid from the Country. Published in *Kernow*, 1934.

D. R. Evans (Gwas Cadok – Servant of Cadock) 188?–197?

A Welsh-speaking Welshman, he came to Cornwall as Vicar of St Merryn. He learned Cornish, became active in Padstow Old Cornwall Society, and was elected its Recorder. He preached powerful sermons in Cornish and translated parts of the Bible into the language. In 1949 he was made a Bard of the Gorseth and served a term as Deputy Grand Bard.

An Vorvran/The Cormorant. Published in *An Lef Kernewek*, 1953.
Enef Car/The Soul of a Friend. Published in *An Lef Kernewek*, 1959.

W. C. D. Watson (Tyrvap – Son of the Land) 188?–196?

William Charles David Watson was one of the original Bards of the Cornish Gorseth initiated by the Archdruid Pedrog at Treorci, in the Rhondda Valley, in 1928. They formed the nucleus of the Gorseth formally set up at Boscawen Un in Cornwall the following year. He was generally regarded as one of the finest speakers of Cornish this century.

My a Glew/I Hear, Carol Kelinen Sans Day/ Sans Day Carol, Covyon Keltek/Celtic Memories. Manuscripts c.1935. Papers of Robert Morton Nance, Courtney Library, Royal Institution of Cornwall, Truro.

A. S. D. Smith (Caradar – Friend of Birds)1883–1950

Language teacher, author of popular textbooks of both Cornish and Welsh and editor of Kernow (1933–4), the first all-Cornish periodical. Well-known for his popular *Welsh Made Easy*, he adopted similar methods for *Cornish Made Easy*, which is still in print. This book, and the supplements published by E.G.R. Hooper, constitute an unsurpassed description of Middle Cornish. Unlike Jenner and Morton Nance, he opposed the use of Early Modern elements in the modern language. His *Trystan hag Ysolt* is the most important modern literary work in Cornish.

Henry Jenner/Henry Jenner. Written c.1935. Publised *An Lef*, 1955.
An Gwlascarer/The Patriot; *An Mytyn Warlergh/The Morning after*; *Ysolt Ow-Tos Dhe Gernow/Isolt Coming to Cornwall.* Written c.1935. Papers of Robet Morton Nance, Courtney Library, Royal Institution of Cornwall, Truro.
An Dasserghyans Kernewek/The Cornish Revival. Written c.1935. Published in *An Lef Kernewek*, 1957.

L. R. Moir (Car Albanek – Scottish Friend) 1890–1983

Leonard Rae Moir was a Scot by birth who served in the Duke of Cornwall's Light Infantry during the First World War. He married a Cornish woman and settled in Cornwall.

An Map Dyworth an Yst/The Boy from the East. Published by the author, 1965.
Gwythoryon an Eglos –An Eglos/The Guardians of the Church – The Church and *Gwythoryon an Eglos – Spyryusoyon an Vengledhyoryon/Guardians of the Church – The Spirits of the Quarrymen* were published by the author, 1969.
Whethel an Cor Kernewek/The Tale of the Cornish Dwarf. This extract published in *Old Cornwall*, 1968.

Robert Victor Walling (Scryfer an Mor – Writer of the Sea) 1890–1976

Walling was a journalist who specialised in nautical subjects. He learnt Cornish from Jenner's *Handbook* and also read widely in contemporary Welsh and Breton literature. During the First World War he served in the Royal Garrison Artillery. While in hospital he produced a beautifully illustrated manuscript magazine , *An Housledhas* (*The West*), which contains a variety of stories, essays and translations of Celtic poetry.

War Lerch an Bresel/After the War. Manuscript c.1916.

Edwin Chirgwin (Map Melyn – Son of the Mill) 1892–1960

Historian, folklorist and influential teacher who helped countless children acquire the elements of the language. He expanded the range of Cornish poetry from a somewhat self-conscious concern with the legendary past and laid the foundation for the flowering of Cornish verse after the Second World War. He wrote stories, essays and sermons in Cornish as well as translating parts of the Bible. His *Rustic Jottings*, as he called his notes on a wide range of observations almost constitute an encyclopedia of Cornwall.

Avon Rejerrah/Rejerrah River. Written c.1925. Published in *An Lef Kernewek*, 1961.
Dhe Hanternos/ At Midnight; Dhe'n Awhesyth/To the Lark; An Jynjy Gesys dhe Goll/The Abandoned Engine House. Published in *Kernow*, 1934.
Gibraltar/Gibraltar. Written c.1941. Published in *An Lef Kernewek*, 1961.

Edmund Henry Hambly (Gwas Arthur – Servant of Arthur) 189? – 197?
Close associate of Robert Morton Nance. Active in the movement Tyr ha Tavas. His personal library now forms part of the Cornish Studies Library in Redruth.

Dew Genes, a Gernow/God Be with You, Cornwall. Published in *Kernow*, 1933.
Mebyon Kernow/Sons of Cornwall. Published in *An Lef Kernewek*, 1973.

David Watkins (Carer Brynyow – Lover of Hills) 1892–1969
A native of Glamorganshire, he graduated at Aberystwyth and went to teach in Cornwall, where he met Jenner and Nance. A member of the Welsh Gorsedd, he became a member of the Cornish Gorseth in 1961. He also served as an early, much-valued member of the Cornish Language Board. Watkins completed Caradar's unfinished *Trystan hag Ysolt.*

Tarth an Jeth/The Break of Day. Published in *An Lef Kernewek*, 1966.
Spyrys an Meneth a Lever y Gevrynyow/The Spirit of the Mountain Tells its Secrets. Published in *An Lef Kernewek*, 1972.

Wilfred Bennetto (Abransek – Bushy-Browed One) 1902–1994
Author, under the name Melville Bennetto, of the first full-length novel published in Cornish, *An Gurun Wosek a Geltya* (*The Bloody Crown of Celtia*)

Bedwyr, Po an Balores Dhewetha/Bedivere, or the Last Chough. Published in *An Lef Kernewek*, 1969.

Margaret Pollard (Arlodhes Ywerdhon – Lady of Ireland)1903–1996
A relative of W.E. Gladstone, she was widely read in the Classics and a scholar of ancient Indian languages. As well as *The Shell Guide to Cornwall*, she wrote some startling verse dramas of which only one, *Beunans Alysaryn*, has been printed.

Gwersyow/Verses. Written c.1939. Published in *An Lef Kernewek*, 1969.
Arlodhes Ywerdhon/The Lady of Ireland. Written c.1939. Published in *An Lef Kernewek*, 1964.

E.G.R. Hooper (Talek – Big-Browed One) 1906 – 1998
Hooper founded the first schools to teach Cornish as part of the curriculum. His thirty-year editorship of *An Lef* enabled many poets to develop their technique and to widen the range of themes encompassed by Coirnish poetry.

A Pena Prydyth/If I Were a Poet. Published in *An Lef*, 1952
Mebyon Kernow/Sons of Cornwall. Published in *An Lef Kernewek*, 1965.
[Pup Comolen]/[Every Cloud]. Published in *An Lef Kernewek, 1967.*

E. E. Morton Nance (Gwas Gwethnok – Servant of Gwethnok) 1909–

Nephew of Robert Morton Nance.

An Brythen Kernewek/The Cornish Tartan. Published by the author, 1960s.

Hilda Ivall (Morvran – Cormorant) 1910–

Member of a talented family which has contributed to many different aspects of Cornish culture. As well as writing poetry in both Cornish and English, she has experimented with abstract painting, making use of the colours of the rocks of Cornwall.

Peder Can Ver: II/Four Short Songs: II. Manuscript c.1970. Collection of the author.
Nebes Gwersyow: I/Some Poems: I. Manuscript c.1974. Collection of the author.
Nebes Gwersyow: II/Some Poems II. Manuscript c.1974. Collection of the author.

Tomás Mac Neacaill (Gwas Kendern – Son of Kentigern) 191?–197?

Irish by birth Mac Neacaill contributed to the journal *Amser Keltek* (*Celtic Time*). He lived for many years in Britain.

An Venen Goth/The Old Woman. Published in *An Lef*, 1953.

Frederick MacDowall (Map Estren Du – Son of the Black Stranger) 191?–197?

A Scot who adopted Cornwall as his homeland.

An Gok/The Cuckoo and *Tanow Yowynkneth/Fires of Youth.* Published in *An Lef,* 1953.

Helena Charles (Maghteth Boudycca – Handmaiden of Boudicca) 1911–1997

Campaigner for rights of national minorities and one of the founders of Mebyon Kernow. She encouraged the performance of Cornish dramas and organised residential courses, where Tony Snell, Richard Gendall and Richard Jenkin and others met.

[A Varrak Ker]/[Dear Knight]. Published in *An Lef*, 1952.

Phoebe Procter (Morwennol – Sea Swallow) 1912–

Daughter of Robert Morton Nance, and audience of many of his poems and stories. She contributed to *Kernow*, but these are the only two of her poems to have survived.

Pyu a Wor an Den a-Garaf?/Who Knows the Man I Love; An Gwaynten/The Spring. Manuscripts c.1935. Papers of Robert Morton Nance, Courtney Library, Royal Institution of Cornwall, Truro.

Harold Edey (Peder an Mor – Peter of the Sea) 1913–

A member of Tyr ha Tavas, he held a chair in accounting at the London School of Economics.

Can Warlergh 'An Balores' (Mordon)/The Chough (after Mordon). Published in *Kernow,* 1933.

Margaret Norris (Brosyores – Embroideress) 192?–

Joined the Gorseth during the Second World War.

Poldice/Poldice. Published in *Aimsir Cheilteach*, 1948.

Richard Gendall (Gelvynak – Curlew) 1924–

Taking an interest in Cornish from an early age, he founded *An Lef* (later *An Lef Kernewek*) and several other periodicals in the language. A language teacher by profession, he has written important textbooks, grammars and dictionaries. His *Kernewek Bew* (1972) was the first Cornish textbook to incorporate modern pedagogical principles, and also to reinforce the importance of the Early Modern period as an element in the contemporary language. Recently, he has championed the merits of Early Modern Cornish as the basis for the Modern literary standard, and has recast his poetic output in accordance with these principles. The poems included in this anthology have all been revised by tthe author, 1999.

Hendrez Diures/An Exile's Dream. Published in *An Lef*, 1951.
Nadelack Looan!/Happy Christmas! Published in *An Lef*, 1952.
Perave an Gunneau/I Prefer the Downs. Published in *An Lef Kernewek*, 1956.
Leesteevan/Launceston. Published in *An Lef Kernewek*, 1956.
An Jowhall/The Jewel; Soon Gen Minfel/A Charm with Yarrow; Tectar/Beauty and *Pandrama?/What Shall I Do?* From the record *Crowdy Crawn* with Brenda Wootton,1973.
Cles?/Comfortable? Manuscript c.1970. Collection of the author.
Pew A Ore?/Who Knows? From the record *Crowdy Crawn*, 1973.
Dirrians Nature/The Survival of Nature; An Ennis/The Island; Whela Ve/Seek Me. Manuscripts c.1970. Collection of the author.

Richard Jenkin (Map Dyvroeth – Son of Exile) 1925–

He and his wife, Ann Trevenen, published and edited the ground-breaking discussion magazine *New Cornwall*, and currently he is editor of the literary magazine *Delyow Derow*.

Pask/Easter. Collection of the author.

Jon Mirande (An Menedhor – The Mountaineer) 1926–1972

Polyglot scholar, writer and Basque nationalist.

Avar Kens Vora/Early Before Morning and *Dewheles a Wra/They Will Return* published in *An Lef Kernewek*, 1955.

R.M. Royle (Pendenhar – Pendenhar) 1926–

Journalist and historian, a former editor of the *Cornish Guardian*.

Cornel Kernow/A Corner of Cornwall; An Edhen Dhu/The Black Bird and *Dus Dhym/Come To Me.* Published in *An Lef Kernewek*, 1972.

Goulven Pennaod (Cadvan – Cadvan) 1928–

Breton scholar, linguist and author. As well as writing poetry and fiction in his own language, he has written short stories in Cornish and a grammar of Middle Cornish.

Gwyns Ha Glaw/Wind and Rain. Published in *An Lef Kernewek*, 1959.

Donald Rawe (Scryfer Lanwednoc – Writer of Padstow) 1930–

Born in Padstow in 1930. He has published various books on Cornish history and topography. He was made a Bard of the Gorseth in 1970.

Can Os Cres/Song of Middle Age. Published in *Cornish Nation*, 1973.
An Lowarnes/The Vixen. Manuscript c.1975. Collection of the author.

W. Morris (Haldreyn – Moor of Thorns) 1937–

One of the original members of the Cornish Language Board.

Keresyk/Little Sweetheart. Published in *An Lef Kernewek,* 1969.
Cucow Bretonek yn Porth Kernewek/Breton Boats in a Cornish Port. Published in *An Lef Kernewek*, 1965.

J.A.N. Snell (Gwas Kevardhu – December's Man) 1938–
Widely travelled, Tony Snell has assimilated many influences and has studied the craft of the early Celtic poets as a model for disciplined metrical and conceptual work.

Mys Dhu/November. Manuscript c.1955. Collection of the author.
An Helgh/The Hunt. Manuscript c.1956. Revised and published in *An Lef*, 1956.
Pyu a Vyn Prena Breten?/Who Will Buy Britain? Manuscript c.1974.Published in *An Lef Kernewek*, 1983.
An Lef Mes a'n Mor/The Voice from the Sea. Manuscript c.1974. Collection of the author.
Chy War an Als/House on the Cliff. Manuscript c.1976. Collection of the author.
Jonathan/Jonathan. Manuscript c.1975. Collection of the author.
An Ros/The Wheel. Manuscript c.1980. Collection of the author.

N.J.A. Williams (Golvan – Sparrow) 1942–
Celtic scholar who has taught at Liverpool University and University College, Dublin, he has published several works in the field of Irish studies. Disappointed by the apparent lack of progress of Cornish, he stopped writing it for some years. More recently, he has proposed reshaping the literary language on the model of the Cornish of the Tudor period.

[Lowsys yu Logh Lagas Glas]/[Dulled is the Lake of a Blue Eye]. Published in *An Lef*, 1962.
[Marthus Bras yu Margh Bryntyn]/[Wondrous Great is a Noble Stallion]. Published in *An Lef Kernewek,*
[Gwaynten 'ma yn Breten Vyghan]/[It is Spring in Brittany]. Published in *An Lef Kernewek*, 1982.
[Bryntyn o Breten ow Thas]/[Noble was the Britain of My Father]. Manuscript c. 1965. Collection of the author.
Kynyaf/Autumn. Manuscript c. 1965. Collection of the author.
Dhe Gof Mordon/In Memory of Mordon. Published in *An Lef Kernewek*, 1973.
Scusow/Shadows. Published in *An Lef Kernewek*, 1965.
Nyns yu ma's Ges a wraf/I'm Only Making Fun. Manuscript c. 1965. Collection of the author.
Maylura/Maylura. Manuscript c. 1960. Collection of the author.

Julyan Holmes (Blew Melen – Yellow-Haired One) 1948–
In addition to poetry and songs, he has written scholarly works on subjects as wide-ranging as Cornish place-names and the medieval prophesies attributed to Merlin.

Kerth Kernowyon/Cornishmen's March. Published in *An Lef Kernewek*, 197

Tim Saunders (Bardh Gwerin – People's Poet) 1952–
Tim Saunders spent his childhood in Cornwall. He studied Celtic Studies at the University College of Wales, Aberystwyth and has published poetry, journalism and fiction in Welsh, Irish and Breton, as well as in Cornish. He lives in Cardiff.

Hunrosen/Dream Rose. Manuscript, 1972. Collection of the author.
Kasa ha Kara/Loving and Hating. Manuscript, 1972. Collection of the author.
Drolla/Tale. Manuscript, 1974. Collection of the author.

Notes

John Davey

Crankan/Cranken

1   Cranken was a somewhat barren farm in Gulval. The message of the poem is that one dollop of fertiliser from a horse on the road out of Penzance will yield far more than the whole of poor Cranken.

2   An alternative name for Marazion (derived from the Cornish for 'Thursday Market'), the town facing St. Michael's Mount.

Georg Sauerwein

Edwin Norris/Edwin Norris

1   Edwin Norris (1795–1872) was a brilliant orientalist employed by the East India Company. His *The Ancient Cornish Drama* (1859) includes the first printed edition of the *Ordinalia* and a grammar of the language.

2   A pun on the name Edwin. 'Edwyn' is the third person singular of the Welsh 'to know'.

3   This refers to the three most familiar prefixes to surnames in Cornwall.
Cowth Ker, dhe Dhen Claf/Dear Friend, to a Sick Man

4   Possibly also addressed to Norris.

Henry Jenner

Bro Goth Agan Tasow/Ancient Land of Our Fathers

1   An adaptation of the Welsh national anthem *Hen Wlad fy Nhadau*.
An Pemthak Pell/The Fifteen Bezants

2   The Archangel Michael has for centuries been regarded as the patron saint of Cornwall. Jenner here links the Cornish coat of arms, the Fifteen Bezants, with the Fifteen Mysteries of the Rosary. A bezant is a gold coin, first struck in Byzantium.
Can Wlascar Agan Mamvro/Patriotic Song of the Motherland

3   Jenner links the Cornish saints with the Knights of the Round Table and also with the Cornish Regiments that supported Charles I.

L.R. Duncombe-Jewell

Mychternes, Mychternes an Eleth Dhus!/Queen, Queen of Angels, Come!

1   Crows-an-Wra . 'The Witch's Cross' is a carved stone cross not far from Land's End.

Robert Morton Nance

Nyns yu Marow Maghtern Arthur!/King Arthur Is Not Dead!

1   It was Morton Nance who popularised the chough as a symbol of the Cornish spirit. A widespread legend had it that Arthur returned in the guise of a chough to guard the coasts.

2   This expression is in Breton.

W.C.D. Watson

Carol Kelinen Sans Day/The Sans Day Carol

1   Refers to a traditional carol associated with the parish of St. Day. Judging by the use of Jenner's spelling and the style of language, this poem must have been written before 1928.
Covyon Keltek/Celtic Memories

2   'The Stone of Writing', a megalithic monument in Penwith.

3   Names recorded in ancient funerary inscriptions in Cornwall.

4   Commemorated on a memorial stone at Carnsew, near Hayle in Penwith.

A.S.D. Smith

Henry Jenner/Henry Jenner

1   The bardic name of Henry Jenner.
An Dasserghyans Kernewek/The Cornish Revival

2   'Land and Language', a patriotic youth movement before the Second World War.

L.R. Moir

An Map Dyworth an Yst/The Boy from the East

1 Joseph of Arimathea.

Edwin Chirgwin

Dhe Hanternos/At Midnight

1 One of the earliest examples of blank verse in Cornish.

Avon Rejerrah/The Rejerrah River

2 This little river runs into the sea by Penhale Sands.

3 Identified with Gwbert, of Dyfed in west Wales.

David Watkins

Tarth an Jeth/The Break of Day

1 After the Welsh of Sir John Morris-Jones (*Toriad Dydd* in his *Caniadau*).

E.G.R. Hooper

Mebyon Kernow/Sons of Cornwall

1 Michael Joseph the Smith (14?? –1497) of St. Keverne was exectuted at Tyburn for leading the Great Rising of 1497. Since the Second World War he has become an icon of Cornish identity.

Tomás Mac Neacaill

An Venen Goth/the Old Woman

1 The Cornish language is personified as an old woman.

Harold Edey

An Balores(Can Warlergh Mordon)/The Chough (After Mordon)

1 Mordon is the bardic name of Robert Morton Nance.

Margaret Norris

Poldice/Poldice

1 The name of a valley near St. Day.

Richard Gendall

Whela Ve/Seek Me

1 The name in Cornish of St. Michael's Mount means 'The Grey Rock in the Wood'.

2 The name of the magical boar that Arthur and his men hunted all the way from Wales to Cornwall.

3 A reference to the Great Rising of 1497.

N.J.A Williams

Dhe Gof Mordon/In Memory of Mordon

1 Mordon is the bardic name of Robert Morton Nance.

Scusow/Shadows

2 A play on words: *scusow* literally means 'shadows', but is also understood as 'anxiety, dread'.

Nyns yu Ma's Ges a Wraf/I'm Only Making Fun

3 Priest in the reign of Mary (1553–8), opponent of the Reformation.

Maylura/Maylura

4 Howel and Alwar were Cornish princes during the Age of Saints.